Sex Roles, Women's Work, and Marital Conflict

University of Plymouth Library

Subject to status this item may be renewed
via your Voyager account

http://voyager.plymouth.ac.uk

Exeter tel: (01392) 475049
Exmouth tel: (01395) 255331
Plymouth tel: (01752) 232323

Sex Roles, Women's Work, and Marital Conflict

A Study of Family Change

John Scanzoni
University of North Carolina

Lexington Books
D.C. Heath and Company
Lexington, Massachusetts
Toronto

Library of Congress Cataloging in Publication Data

Scanzoni, John H. 1935-
  Sex roles, women's work, and marital conflict.

  1. Family. 2. Sex role. 3. Women—Employment. I. Title.
HQ728.S286   301.42   78-58981
ISBN 0-669-02400-7

0074793

Published simultaneously in Canada.

Printed in the United States of America.

International Standard Book Number: 0-669-02400-7

Library of Congress Catalog Card Number: 78-58981

108751   301.42
              ScA

Contents

List of Figures

List of Tables

Preface

Changing gender-role preferences, employment for women, and conflict and negotiation within the marriage relationship are all current topics of great interest. However, little attention has been given to their interconnections. In this book, the links are made via an eclectic version of cost-reward theory. In the early 1970s, some spokepersons were alleging that radical innovations in the character of marriage and family spelled the end of traditional domestic patterns. By the middle and late 1970s, the pendulum had swung the other way, and some observers were arguing that reports on the death of the traditional family had been "greatly exaggerated." This book treads the middle ground between these two extreme positions. I try to explore the nature of the current evolution or development of marital patterns. The organizing principle of the book is the sex-role preferences held by women (as well as men).

My central argument is that these elements lie at the core of marital/familial change. Sex roles can be said to indicate the kinds of preferences, goals, interests, or rewards that women seek. Evidence presented in the following chapters from a representative sample of married women shows that women who prefer egalitarian marital arrangements define their work as a right, whereas women whose sex-role preferences are traditional are more likely to regard employment as an option.

Likewise, egalitarian women make a more significant impact on family lifestyle, social class position, and the sharing of household duties—including being coproviders with their husbands. These impacts are, in part, due to the greater levels of both tangible and intangible resources egalitarian women possess.

Finally, egalitarian women, who define work as a right and for whom it has important consequences, are also more likely to be more effective negotiators and to have greater bargaining power with their husbands. If changes are actually occurring within modern marriages, then they must be identifiable in the ways in which wives engage in decision processes with husbands to arrive at what wives want from marriage, their husbands, their occupations, and from other sources as well.

Implications for social policy are explained in the light of a particular question generated by these ongoing changes: If, indeed, women are coming to prefer more egalitarian or individualistic interests, will this trend inevitably have negative consequences for marriage and family as institutions? Will group interests be sacrificed for individual interests? My argument is that such an either/or dichotomy is not necessarily valid. Instead, I suggest that healthier or stronger marital patterns are likely to emerge when women's interests are negotiated in a context of justice, equity, and maximum joint profit.

Acknowledgments

Many people contributed to this effort, and I am indebted to all of them, both named and unnamed. Letha Scanzoni originally suggested the idea of a follow-up study and edited parts of the manuscript. Lucy Stone and Karen File supervised the data-collection stage, while Lynda Kyrk managed the task of coding and data reduction. Lois Downey provided invaluable counsel during data analyses and functioned as an extraordinarily skillful programmer. The ideas governing the finished product emerged from numerous discussions over the years with a variety of colleagues. I am especially grateful for the criticisms and insights supplied by Gary LaFree, Karen Polonko, William Strahle, and Maximiliane E. Szinovacz, each of whom read various segments of the several versions through which this and related manuscripts passed. The entire research project was supported by U.S. Public Health Service Grant RO 3 MH28501.

1 Overview

Introduction

Trying to make sense of contemporary marriage is no simple task. The popular press and scholars agree that the institutions of marriage and family are changing. That conclusion seems obvious. However, in spite of overwhelming concurrence that something is happening, there has not been a great deal of systematic research to verify the allegedly obvious.

Use of demographic data has been one way the question of change has been broached. Very often the media will use such information to discuss increases in the proportions of married women who work or decreases in the numbers of children women are having.

> Divorce statistics are featured in the evening telecasts; Sunday Supplements dwell on unwed motherhood; and living together makes the cover of a national news weekly. The traditional family life cycle circumscribed by marriage and childbearing, it would seem, is going out of style (Glick and Norton, 1977:3).

Responsible demographic descriptions, such as those of Glick and Norton or Bane (1976), suggest the virtues and limits of that kind of work. A virtue is that, based on either large, carefully drawn national samples, or else on a total census, it is possible after the fact to describe shifts in the composition of the population. These shifts include proportions of men or women who do or do not marry, whether they are marrying at earlier or later ages, whether more persons are sharing households who are not legally married, and so forth. It is vitally important that such data continue to be used to determine change or constancy among what Merton (1957:299) calls aggregates or collectivities within the population.

Unfortunately, the limits are that most of the documentation occurs after the fact; demographic predictions pertaining to marriage and family are not known for their reliability. What is even more significant is that many demographers seem to give little energy and attention to the development of theoretical explanations of the collectivities they are analyzing. Goldscheider's (1971) thoughtful work is a notable exception, and there are other demographers who do pay attention to theory (see *Social Forces*, September 1975). It is interesting, however, that very often when demographers do attempt to

1

theorize about aggregate phenomena (for example, the correlation between the proportion of women who work and the proportion who are well educated), they leave that aggregate level and turn instead to characteristics of individuals to explain the association (such as tastes and preferences) (compare Westoff, 1978). In other words, in most instances demographers have not been able to use aggregate variables to explain aggregate phenomena.

Preferences

The general inability of demographers to develop theoretical explanations in no way invalidates the importance of tastes or preferences to explain why individuals behave as they do. Indeed, Homans (1974) argues that there is no more valid way to achieve understanding of social processes and social structures. Furthermore, according to Coleman (1975) an increasing number of social scientists (sociologists, economists, anthropologists, psychologists, political scientists) are coming to share that conviction. I happen to be one of them, and my aim in this book is to show how those ideas help us understand and explain persistence and change in certain key aspects of contemporary marriage. I also hope to point toward ways in which valid predictions can be made about future marriage patterns.

Unlike demographers, however, I am working at what Coleman (1975) and others call the level of microsociology. As will be elaborated, I am persuaded that a much more basic understanding of fundamental family changes can be obtained by focusing on marriage as a social group than by looking at aggregates of persons or families.[1]

Marriage as a two-person group falls under the heading of microsociology, as do other groups of similar and somewhat larger sizes. Size is one variable that distinguishes microsociology from macrosociology, since with size comes certain additional considerations. For instance, as Rubin and Brown (1975) point out, there are many principles that apply to negotiations between husbands and wives that also apply to negotiations between labor and management representatives. But in the latter case there are additional considerations, such as the fact that each side consists of more than one person who is negotiating.

Furthermore, these opponents must consider not only their own personal interests but also and primarily the interests of the groups they represent. While it could be argued that both these complexities might sometimes be present in marital negotiations to a certain degree, their presence is not as readily apparent.

The terms referred to earlier, taste and preference, while not unknown to sociologists, are not as widely utilized as their synonyms, such as goal, interest, and desired reward. These latter concepts are commonly used in connection with a variety of theoretical perspectives or conceptual approaches known variously as exchange, conflict, power, cost-reward, equity, and so forth. While all of these approaches have distinctive heritages and assumptions, and have often been applied to different kinds of substantive phenomena, they all share certain basic assumptions.

My aim in this book is to build on the common ground that exists among these several kinds of theoretical perspectives in order to understand and explain three kinds of issues in contemporary marriage: changes in the *meaning* of work to women; changes in the *consequences* of women's work, and finally, changes in the ways in which women *negotiate* or conflict with their husbands. But before moving into the next four chapters, where I discuss the significance of these questions and also how I probe them, we must first give some attention to the eclectic synthesis of reward-cost theory that will be applied to the analyses of those three questions.

A Reward-Cost Approach

Ellis (1971) contends that there are two solutions to the "problem of order," that is, why groups form, persist, change, and dissolve. One is the functionalist or normative solution: people behave as they do primarily because they have learned that certain norms are appropriate and thus they feel a moral obligation to conform. Coser (1976:154) argues that, in modern sociology, that viewpoint is becoming eclipsed.

Among increasingly popular candidates to replace the moral-obligation approach is the second solution cited by Ellis, which he calls "utilitarianism," a label that unfortunately may carry certain negative nuances. Nevertheless, that label subsumes each of the above approaches since all of them concur in the basic assumption that *persons and groups behave as they do in order to gain rewards and avoid costs.*

It is this constant pursuit of interests, goals, tastes, and preferences that gives rise to marriages. Persons form groups called marriage because they cannot otherwise get what they want, or as much of what they want. Similarly, the marriage groups will persist as long as both parties believe that the ratio of rewards to costs is favorable relative to what they could experience outside the association. Also, the arrangements or patterns of the marriage group will change in order to permit one or both parties to experience greater rewards and fewer costs. Finally, marriages dissolve when costs outweigh rewards relative to potential external situations.

Intrinsic to all four group issues and to utilitarian theory is some form of negotiation or bargaining. (Some might prefer the label *decision making*.) Both Chadwick-Jones (1976) and Rubin and Brown (1975) acknowledge that in the literature there are technical differences between negotiation and bargaining. However, the distinctions are very difficult to maintain, and Rubin and Brown in particular prefer to use the terms interchangeably, as do I. They define bargaining as "the process whereby two or more parties attempt to settle what each shall give and take, or perform and receive, in a transaction between them" (p. 2).

Thus, in terms of the four issues cited, spouses may first of all negotiate the initial terms of their group formation. For instance, the woman, Sandra, may at the time of marriage say to her husband, Fred, "I would like you to be the one in charge of meal preparation"; or "My job requires me to be away three evenings a week, so I can't compromise." Parenthetically, many couples may not negotiate certain elements during early marriage. Particularly if they are what later in this chapter I call "sex-role-traditional," both spouses may take for granted, without any negotiation, what each is supposed to "give and take" or "perform and receive" in terms of employment, household duties, sex, and so forth. Fox (1974) describes those situations as "spontaneous consensus," while Brickman (1974) labels them as "fully structured" arrangements. Such arrangements are not questioned by the parties involved; it is simply accepted that certain behaviors are expected of wives, others of husbands.

Second, those initial exchanges, whether negotiated or arrived at spontaneously, tend to persist as long as both parties define them as equitable (Walster and Walster, 1975). *Equity* or *justice* simply means they perceive the arrangement as fair; in other words, each party believes he or she is receiving the right amounts of benefits from it relative to what each is contributing. Should feelings of inequity develop about the arrangement, there is likely to be an attempt on the part of one or both parties to negotiate change—the third group issue.

All negotiations, as Rubin and Brown (1975:18) indicate, stem from a divergence or conflict of interests. If there were no divergence, there would be no reason to negotiate. Let us assume that Fred has been cooking each night for one year and has not considered it unfair to have Sandra away three evenings. But for a variety of reasons he alters his preferences or goals. He no longer wants to cook on the nights his wife is home. He considers the present arrangement unfair. He then raises the issue with his wife and she immediately agrees to conform to his new preferences. Or she could negotiate with him for a period of time and attempt, through a series of offers and counteroffers, to arrive at a compromise that also involves such other issues as food shopping and cleaning.

These two alternative routes (her immediate response versus protracted decision-making processes) have been conceptualized as implicit versus explicit bargaining (Chadwick-Jones, 1976:108-111). One could hypothesize (especially in what are defined as sex-role-traditional marriages) that a good deal of marital bargaining is implicit in the sense that few if any counteroffers are made in response to an original proposal or offer. Sometimes the response is not even verbal—a nod, an indifferent look, a shrug, a smile, and so forth, indicate implicit assent. Or it may be verbal—"I don't care either way." In our illustration, the wife's first response was implicit, her second was explicit bargaining (Chertkoff and Esser, 1976), that is, an overt and self-conscious effort consisting of several offers and counteroffers to rearrange their exchanges over particular matters.

Deutsch (1973) points out that negotiation, or conflicts of interest, can be pursued in at least two ways. One he calls constructive, or cooperative; the other he calls destructive, or competitive. In our illustration, the spouses can negotiate their divergence or disagreement so as to arrive at a resolution that each considers just. They have achieved a new "fair exchange." Conversely, their negotiations can result, not in resolution, but in what Dahrendorf (1959) calls regulation of the conflict. Actor imposes a settlement that Other thinks is unfair, but Other lacks (or considers it too costly to use) power to get Actor to change.

Recall that this discussion of negotiation is directed toward explaining how groups such as marriage change their arrangements. And at least since Simmel, sociologists have been aware that conflicts resulting in equitable changes have positive consequences for persistence of a group. However, the presence of numerous regulated marital conflicts presumably contributes to the likelihood of dissolution (separation/divorce). What has not been researched is how many regulated conflicts (and over what issues) are likely to stimulate dissolution—the fourth group issue.

For that matter, as Rubin and Brown (1975) observe, very little research has been done outside the laboratory on the dynamics of negotiation and conflict processes. The work of Raush et al. (1974) is one exception, and there are some others, but by and large the dynamics of these ongoing marital processes in actual settings have seldom been investigated or apprehended. In spite of the fact that bargaining processes are central to utilitarian theories (exchange, conflict, and so forth), they have largely been ignored.

Perhaps the most apparent reason for this state of affairs is the difficulty inherent in conceptualizing and quantifying processes, and in collecting valid data on them. That is not to say that in recent years studies of family have ignored exchange theory (Nye, 1978; Scanzoni, 1970, 1972, 1977) or conflict theory (Straus, 1976; Sprey, 1969, 1971) or power, which is intrinsic to both exchange and conflict notions (Cromwell and Olson, 1975). But virtually all the work in these areas has tended to focus on the end products, the outcomes, the deals, the consensuses, the fair exchanges, or the regulated conflicts at which couples have finally arrived at by the time the researcher collects data from them. Among the scholars cited, Sprey has perhaps been most explicit about the need to study processes of offers and counteroffers, threats and promises, and so on, that result in either regulated conflicts or consensuses.

We moved into this brief survey of utilitarian theory because the argument was made that this was the best (most valid) way to understand and explain certain contemporary marital changes. (Coleman, 1975, prefers the term *purposive action* as a general construct to subsume notions of exchange, conflict, power; I shall use *utilitarian, reward-cost,* and *purposive action* interchangeably.) Of necessity, I have omitted a great many details about utilitarian theory, some of which are available in the sources already cited and others elsewhere (Scanzoni, 1978, 1979c).

In addition, the following chapters will elaborate certain aspects of reward-cost theory as it applies to the meanings and consequences of women's work, and also to processes of marital conflict. My argument will be that these three issues are absolutely central to any consideration of fundamental changes in marital structures.

Sex Roles as Preferences

To probe these questions, we must first think about the matter of preferences, tastes, desired rewards, costs to avoid, goals, interests and so on. What goals did women and men seek from each other (through what is called marriage) fifty, twenty, or ten years ago? What goals do they seek now or will they seek five, ten, or twenty years hence? It is readily apparent that if goals change, group patterns are also likely to change. If college students come to prefer job-oriented education over liberal-arts education, then many colleges will probably change to accommodate those goals. If men come to expect that wives should support them financially, then marriage patterns will be likely to shift accordingly. The research question is: Where does one look to assess marital preferences or goals? How does one identify them?

Holter's (1970) response is to look at that construct known as sex role or gender role. While psychologists may look at it somewhat differently (compare Bem, 1977), Holter contends that to sociologists sex role is essentially a set of preferences, rewards, tastes, and goals that a person learns because he or she happens to be male or female. The literature suggests that these are learned from parents during childhood and adolescence, but as I shall demonstrate, they are by no means rigidly fixed in any functionalist sense. They are not idiosyncratic to an individual; rather, they are shared conceptions of the desirable or undesirable.

Several studies to be cited have sought to measure these preferences using items similar to those displayed in figure 1-1. Often items such as these are called sex-role attitudes, or attitudes about sex role. Although *attitude* is a fairly innocuous term, it is imprecise. As far as the issues before us are concerned, it does not convey as simple and direct a meaning as does the term *preference.* These preferences are desires, wants, or tastes. The preferences for particular goals or "conceptions of the desirable" are not idiosyncratic (as attitudes might be) but are shared by persons and groups. Following Holter (1970) the assumption is made that women and men share preferences regarding a goal labeled *degree of gender role differentiation.* That construct is defined as the degree to which women or men prefer or want or desire gender roles that are egalitarian or interchangeable with regard to the rewards and costs of both occupational and household behaviors.

These preferences lie on a continuum, with some women (and men) preferring a high degree of interchangeability in terms of both sets of behaviors.

Position of Wife

Traditional-Wife Role (TW)

a. A married woman's most important task in life should be taking care of her husband and children.
b. She should realize that a woman's greatest reward and satisfaction come through her children.
d. If she works, she should not try to get ahead in the same way that a man does.
f. A wife should *not* have equal authority with her husband in making decisions.
g. If she has the same job as a man who has to support his family, she should not expect the same pay.
j. A wife should realize that, just as a woman is not suited for heavy physical work, there are also other kinds of jobs she is not suited for, because of her mental and emotional nature.
k. A wife should give up her job whenever it inconveniences her husband and children.
l. If a mother of young children works, it should be only while the family needs the money.

Wife Self-Actualization (SA)

c. Having a job herself should be just as important as encouraging her husband in his job.
e. She should be able to make long-range plans for her occupation, in the same way that her husband does for his.
h. If being a wife and mother isn't satisfying enough, she should take a job.
i. There should be more day care centers and nursery schools so that more young mothers could work.

Position of Husband-Father

Problematic Husband Alterations (PHA)

d. If *her* job sometimes requires her to be away from home overnight, this should not bother him.
e. If a child gets sick and his wife works, he should be just as willing as she to stay home from work and take care of the child.
f. If his wife makes more money than he does, this should not bother him.
h. On the job, men should be willing to work for women supervisors.
i. A married man should be willing to have a smaller family, so that his wife can work if she wants to.

Institutionalized Equality (IE)

b. If his wife works, he should share equally in household chores such as cooking, cleaning, and washing.
c. If his wife works, he should share equally in the responsibilities of child care.

Traditional-Husband Role (TH)

a. A married man's chief responsibility should be his job.
g. The husband should be the head of the family.

Position of Mother

Religious-Legitimation-of-Mother Role (RLM)

a. Do you believe that the institution of marriage and family was established by God?
b. Do you feel that being a mother is a special calling from God?

Traditional-Mother Role (TM)

c. Do you think that a working mother can establish just as warm and secure relationship with her children as a mother who does *not* work?
d. Do you feel that a parent gets more satisfaction when a son gets ahead in his occupation than when a daughter gets ahead in hers?
e. Do you feel that a marriage is *in*complete without children?
f. Do you think that young girls should be permitted as much independence as boys?
g. Do you feel a preschool child is likely to suffer if the mother works?

Figure 1-1. Social Positions of Wife, Husband-Father, and Mother, with Role Dimensions

Persons at that end of the continuum prefer low differentiation or very little sex typing of behaviors. Such women, for instance, want to participate as fully as men in the rewards of occupational involvement (and are willing to bear its costs); and they also want men to participate more fully in the costs of household behaviors and in their gratifications, especially those that come from parenting.

While that end of the continuum is labeled *modern* or *contemporary* in the literature, the other end has often been called *traditional*. (No value judgments are intended by these terms.) A traditional orientation indicates preferences for continued role differentiation between wives and husbands, with occupational and household behaviors being ascribed chiefly on the basis of sex. In short, items such as those in figure 1-1 may be taken to indicate preferences for desired rewards (and acceptable costs) within both occupational and household settings. Thus they are linked with utilitarian theory in that they identify interests or goals that persons hold.

Sometimes the term *preference* is used interchangeably with *norm*, although the latter term is generally broader than the idea of preference. However, when in the following pages I use the term *sex-role norm*, I am using it in this more restricted sense—a preference about what should be in terms of particular costs and rewards. In any case, the label *attitude* will never be used because of the imprecision inherent in linking it with "purposive action" or reward-cost theory.

Evidence of Changing Sex Roles

Several studies suggest that increasing numbers of people are beginning to hold gender-role preferences that are more egalitarian and less traditional than those held by persons some years before. For instance, after examining several separate sample surveys taken from 1964 through 1974, Mason et al. (1976:593-594) conclude that there has been "considerable change in women's sex role attitudes since the mid-1960's. . . . [There has been] a sharp decline in the proportion of women believing that maternal employment is harmful to children's well-being. . . . Women from all walks of life have apparently undergone comparable change since 1964."

Those striking conclusions, from representative samples of American women, are supported by three reports on American college students. Parelius (1975) compared representative samples of students from an eastern women's college in 1969 and again in 1973. She concluded that, over time, "sizeable shifts toward Feminism occurred." The greatest changes in the direction of egalitarianism were in their "attitudes toward work, financial responsibilities, and the division of labor in the home" (1975:51). Parelius also reports that her women respondents did not perceive that men were changing as much as they themselves were.

Bayer analyzed results from several national samples of college students. In one of these samples, the same college freshmen who, in 1967, had been queried regarding women's roles were followed up in 1971 and asked the same question. In 1967, 66 percent of the men and 44 percent of the women were classified as gender-role-traditional. By 1971, the figures had dropped to 30 and 15 percent, respectively.

> Similarly, successive cohorts of the new college students since 1970 have shown declines in endorsement of the "traditional" women's roles and increasing endorsement of sex equality in employment. In 1970 . . . 57 percent of male freshmen and . . . 37 percent of female freshmen endorsed the statement of traditional roles for women . . . (Bayer, 1975:391).

But by 1973, Bayer reports that those figures had declined to 41 and 19 percent, respectively.

A third study compared two different 1971 and 1974 representative samples of never-married white undergraduates from the same midwestern university (Scanzoni, 1976). The findings were similar to those discovered by Parelius and by Bayer. Both sexes showed significant differences over the three-year period in the direction of increased sex-role egalitarianism.

Moreover, at time B (1974) the women were significantly more egalitarian or modern than the men. Also, the amount of change in sex-role preferences exhibited by the women for the three-year period was substantially greater (twice as much) than that revealed by the men.

Therefore, both from household samples of women and from several college samples of both sexes, there is indeed evidence of changes in sex-role preferences. Women in particular, and men to a lesser extent, are coming to adopt less traditional, more egalitarian sex or gender roles. Incidentally, the conclusion that men are less oriented toward egalitarianism than women is also supported by Komarovsky's (1976) work.

The First Study (1971)

In the summer and early fall of 1971 National Analysts cooperated with me in order to interview 3,000 married men and women ranging in (wife's) age from 18 to 44. Both blacks and whites were included in the ten-state survey. We used the items listed in figure 1-1 and came to conclusions about sex-role changes similar to those reported in the preceding citations (Scanzoni, 1975a, 1975b). Younger men and women (ages 18 to 29) tended to be more egalitarian (preferring role interchangeability) than older men and women (ages 30 to 44); women (younger and older) tended to be more egalitarian than men; blacks were less sex-role-traditional than whites. Most powerful and most consistent of all was the finding that better-educated persons (thirteen or more years of school) were more sex-role-egalitarian than were less-educated persons, regardless of sex, race, or age.

The major purpose of the 1971 study was to see if there was any connection between sex roles and fertility control. The literature suggested that women who were less traditional should be able to control their own fertility more effectively. The theoretical reasoning is based directly on utilitarian theory. Children provide numerous intangible rewards and gratifications to both parents. They also provide status to the married woman; a child is a way to show that she has achieved a goal that provides great prestige in the eyes of significant others. (All these rewards can be called "familistic" gratifications.) Simultaneously, children are costly in an obvious economic sense, and also in terms of the time and energy resources of the parent. Since the parent most responsible for childcare usually turns out to be the mother, it is her time/energy resources that are expended.

A woman who is sex-role-modern prefers rewards that are individualistic, that is, tangible and intangible gratifications that she herself gains directly, usually (though not always) through some form of occupational involvement. It was reasoned that since one of the costs of having more children would be less opportunity to pursue their own gratifications, role-modern women should intend to have fewer children overall; should have longer intervals between children; should actually have fewer children; and should be better contraceptors in the sense that they would use methods known to be most effective, and also that they would have experienced fewer contraceptive failures leading to unintended children.

The results turned out as predicted based on reward-cost or utilitarian theory. Younger women who were more role-traditional—who did not want role differentiation or individualistic rewards—were indifferent to the costs of additional numbers of children. Conversely, role-modern women wanted to experience as few of those familistic costs as possible in order to be less impeded in the pursuit of individualistic rewards. Consequently, they practiced more effective fertility control than did traditional women. Also, as expected, women who worked full time were more sex-role-egalitarian than nonworkers, and they also practiced more effective fertility control.

The Second Study (1975 Reinterview)

Underlying the first study was the idea that sex-role preferences exercise prior influence on fertility control and on work behaviors. The theoretical basis for that influence is discussed earlier, but empirically it is an unsettled matter, since all the measures were gathered at the same point in time. In order to have greater confidence that subjectively held sex-role preferences actually influence fertility or work behavior, one would have to have a longitudinal study in which the same persons were interviewed at two different points in time. Therefore, in the summer and fall of 1975, sufficient funds became available to reinterview only the white women who had been ages 18 to 29 at the initial 1971 observation.[2]

One of the purposes of the reinterview was to try to identify any causal influences that 1971 sex roles, work behaviors, and fertility-control behaviors might have had on the very same phenomena during the four-year interval, and also in 1975. The full results of that particular investigation are available elsewhere (Scanzoni, 1979a, 1979b). However, since those findings will be relevant in later chapters, I shall briefly summarize them here.

Women's Work

First, the most common way of describing the fact of women's work is to report whether or not they are employed at the time of the interview. Maret-Havens contends, however, that this method "is not a good measure of women's labor market behavior. Such a measure ignores substantial variations in the character or manner of female labor force participation" (1977:35). She contends that a woman enumerated at time 1 may stop or start working next week, or have been working for three months, three weeks, three days, or seven years. Thus merely asking a woman whether she works "right now" obscures a great deal about the significance of work in her life. To correct this shortcoming, Maret-Havens suggests that we probe the woman's work history. For example, women interviewed in 1975 traced their work involvement for us from that point back through 1971. Table 1-1 shows that, among the women who ever worked at all during

Table 1-1
Number of Months in the Labor Force by Sex, Only among Persons Ever Employed, 1971-1975

Number of Months	Women		Men	
	Percent	*n*	*Percent*	*n*
1-12	18.0	55	0.5	2
13-24	17.6	54	1.2	5
25-36	17.0	52	2.4	10
37-48	11.5	35	4.2	18
49-59	35.9	110	91.7	390
Total	100.0	306	100.0	425
$\bar{x}$ months in labor force	40		58	

that time span, some 36 percent are found in the highest category; that is, they worked as many months as most of the men (92 percent) did.

It is not surprising that almost all husbands worked steadily during that period of time. But it is unexpected that more than a third of their wives worked just as steadily. *Continuity* is what Maret-Havens calls this way of looking at work involvement. Women may rank as high, medium, or low; and of course some wives never worked at all during the interval. Relatively continuous participation in the labor force reflects not only greater seriousness of purpose regarding work, it is also one means toward steady increases in pay, fringe benefits, seniority, security, advancement, and so forth.

For example, Polachek argues that "the major causal factor determining male-female wage differentials" are sex differences in "... continuous work experience. ... The result of this discontinuous labor force participation is that females both enter occupations requiring lesser amounts of training and train less even when in professions typified by much on-the-job training. As a result, we observe females being over-represented in lower-paying occupations while also receiving lower pay in the higher-paying professions" (1975:111).

In short, his argument is that if women displayed as much continuity as men, wage differences would disappear. However, Polachek's conclusions must be tempered by those of Koppel and Appelbaum (1976). They argue that committed women workers earn less than men even when controlling for work experience. Therefore they contend that the wage differentials can be attributed more to economic discrimination against women than to work experience or continuity. Comparison of these two studies is complicated by the fact that Polachek's analyses contain observations covering many more years than do those of Koppel and Appelbaum.

In any case, sexism is one factor that helps explain women's lower earnings. Indeed, job discrimination may become a factor that depresses continuity. That is, some working women may perceive discrimination with regard to wage increments, and thus may leave the labor force because the rewards do not outweigh the costs. Polachek himself acknowledges that continuity may be affected by discrimination, and that it is difficult to separate the two elements (p. 111). Therefore, it should be made explicit that job discrimination and institutional sexism are indeed intertwined with continuity.

Keeping that complication in mind, it turned out that one of the most important positive influences on higher continuity was 1971 sex-role preferences.[3] As a utilitarian or reward-cost framework would lead us to expect, women who in 1971 strongly preferred occupational gratifications took purposive action to gain them, that is, they worked more steadily throughout the following years than women who preferred more traditional rewards. In subsequent chapters, continuity emerges as an important factor related to the meanings of work, its consequences, and also marital conflicts. Thus, continuity is significant because of what it indicates in and of itself, because of what predicts it, and finally because of the impacts it has.

Women's Income

A second set of related findings that becomes significant in later chapters centers around the amount of income that working women earned in 1975, and how much their income has increased since 1971. As might be expected from Polachek's observations, more continuity resulted in higher 1975 earnings. Simultaneously, the more strongly women preferred sex-role interchangeability in 1971, the more money they were earning by 1975. In other words, women with stronger preferences for individualistic attainments at point A were in fact attaining at a higher level (in terms of dollars) at point B. Once again, this is precisely the sort of relationship one would derive from utilitarian theory. If it has any validity in general, and if sex-role preferences are a particular way to assess preferred rewards and unwanted costs, then it can be predicted that women with more modern or individualistic preferences will behave in such a way as to maximize income.

Income is valued, of course, not solely in its tangible senses but also for its potent intangible benefits: sense of worth, identity, perceived respect and esteem, prestige, and power. Men have traditionally sought income for both tangible and intangible reasons. As elaborated more fully in later chapters, one of the most profound changes occurring among women as they become more role-modern or individualistic is a shift from working primarily for tangible benefits ("extra" money to help meet family needs) to working for intangible gratifications as well. As one woman told the interviewer: "Even though I don't need to work, I like to have my own money." In other words, discretionary income earned by her own efforts provided her with a sense of accomplishment and autonomy that went beyond the money itself.

Fertility Patterns

The third array of findings, reported elsewhere, that becomes useful later in this book pertains to fertility patterns. In the past, women who had more children were less likely to work, but it has not been clear whether working "caused" them to have fewer children, or whether having fewer children reduced constraints on working, thus "causing" their work. In distilled form, the conclusions at which I arrived were that in 1971 the more sex-role-modern they were (that is, the more egalitarian and individualistic their preferences), the fewer births they intended to have; and the fewer they intended in 1971, the fewer they actually had by 1975. As indicated earlier, that is the kind of fertility-control sequence one would expect to derive from utilitarian theory.

Changes in Sex Roles

Besides exploring that cluster of questions related to women's labor-force participation, income, and fertility patterns, the 1975 reinterview had an additional major purpose: To what degree, if at all, did the sex roles of these women change? The years between 1971 and 1975 were marked by a great deal of turmoil and change in the political realm (Watergate), the military realm (the sputtering out of the Viet Nam war—the first that America ever "lost"), and the economic realm (the unusual combination of high inflation with high unemployment). Birth rates continued their decline, divorce rates continued upward, though at a somewhat slower pace, and marriage rates, after reaching a peak in 1972, began to decline (Glick and Norton, 1977).

As I noted at the beginning of this chapter, ordinary citizens were very much persuaded that things were "not what they used to be." The Equal Rights Amendment was passed by Congress and rapidly approved by many states. Highly publicized lawsuits were being waged and won by women charging economic, political, and social discrimination. Stories repeatedly appeared in the media about women entering schools and jobs that had formerly been shut tight to females. (Women reporters, for example, appeared frequently on national TV news.) Feminism as a widespread social force seemed to be losing some of the zaniness (bra burnings) of the late sixties that was attached to the label "women's lib." Indeed, that term and the aura of faddishness that surrounded it were being replaced by a growing awareness on the part of large numbers of people that feminism, or the thrust for women's rights, was as much a permanent feature of American life as was the Black movement. That realization in part probably spurred reactions by the extremely conservative forces of Phyllis Schlafly and others against ERA, against a woman's right to choose abortion, and so forth.

These factors, plus the earlier references to sex-role changes, would lead one to predict that by 1975 women should be more sex-role-modern than they were in 1971. That is, their level of preferences for role interchangeability or egalitarianism should have become stronger over time. Table 1-2 reveals that that is indeed what happened among the women interviewed in 1971 and again in 1975, using the items in figure 1-1. They have become more egalitarian regarding the two roles that are part of the position of wife.[4] The first role is the traditional-wife (TW) role, which "can be defined as representing an emphasis in which the interests of husband/children are placed ahead of those of the wife" (Scanzoni, 1975b:29). Thus, by 1975, women became less willing to give husband/child interests as much priority over their own interests as they gave them in 1971. The second role is called self-actualization (SA) and "is defined as one in which wife interests are equal to those of husband and children" (p. 29). By 1975, women believed more strongly than in 1971 that their own interests should have similar priority and significance to those of their families.

Similarly, women have become more egalitarian about the three roles that are part of the position of husband-father.[5] The first of these is problematic husband alterations (PHA), defined as "one in which husband's interests remain basically superior to or more significant than those of the wife, but yet there

Table 1-2
Differences in Sex-Role Modernity,[a] 1971 and 1975
(mean scores: n = 427)

	1971	1975	p
TW[b]	18.10	14.40	.000
SA[c]	9.00	10.42	.000
PHA[c]	9.65	12.10	.000
IE[c]	5.20	6.20	.000
TH[b]	5.00	4.70	.004
RLM[b]	1.67	1.57	.002
TM[b]	2.93	2.10	.000

[a]See figure 1-1 for item wording.

[b]Low score = greater gender modernity.

[c]High score = greater modernity.

exists the live option of temporary incursion into the husband's interests for the sake of wife interests" (Scanzoni, 1975b:37). By 1975 women were more strongly persuaded than in 1971 that such incursions are legitimate and equitable.

The second is institutionalized equality (IE), defined as "one in which the husband's interests are not superior to nor more significant than the interests of his working wife" (p. 38). By 1975, women held these innovative orientations more strongly than they did in 1971. Finally there is the traditional-husband (TH) role, "defined as a form of the 'patriarchal ideology' . . . in which the greater significance of the husband's interests and authority are legitimated in statuses ascribed to him by sex" (p. 38). Women were more prone to reject this orientation in 1975 than they were in 1971.

Finally, women have become more egalitarian regarding the two roles that are part of the position of mother.[6] The first of these dimensions is the religious-legitimation-of-the-mother (RLM) role, "defined as the degree of sacredness attached to marital and familial patterns" (Scanzoni, 1975b:45). Over the years, women in the sample have come to attach less of a sacred aura to the particular marital and familial arrangements that predominate in Western society. The second dimension is the traditional-mother (TM) role, "defined as one in which the interests of children are placed ahead of those of the woman. Mother centered considerations are placed ahead of person-centered or individualistic considerations" (p. 46). Here, too, women were less likely by 1975 to prefer that subordination of their own well-being than they did in 1971. (Table 1-3 shows the correlations among these several role dimensions in 1971 and in 1975.)

Tables 1-4, 1-5, and 1-6 point to the same conclusion as table 1-2, but with more detail as to how wives moved along the continuum from traditional to

Table 1-3
Intercorrelations among Sex-Role Dimensions in 1971 and 1975
(n = 427)

| | 1971[a] | | | | | | | 1975[a] | | | | | |
	TW	SA	PHA	IE	TH	RLM	TM	TW	SA	PHA	IE	TH	RLM	TM
TW[b]		.42	.38	.12	.40	.40	.47		.47	.56	.28	.49	.50	.51
SA			.46	.15	.13	.24	.37			.52	.21	.16	.28	.37
PHA				.22	.12	.26	.32				.38	.32	.36	.37
IE					.04	.02	.12					.18	.22	.18
TH						.21	.26						.35	.34
RLM							.29							.30
TM														

[a]See figure 1-1 for item wording.
[b]All dimensions are coded so that egalitarianism or modernity is high or positive.

Table 1-4
Percentages of Wives by Their Responses to Role Items within Social Position of Wife, 1971 and 1975,[a]
(n = 427)

TW Role

TRADITIONAL → MODERN

| | Strongly Agree | | Agree | | Mixed Feelings | | Disagree | | Strongly Disagree | |
Items[b]	1971	1975	1971	1975	1971	1975	1971	1975	1971	1975
a	51.5	28.1	31.1	41.5	12.4	18.0	3.7	10.1	1.2	2.3
b	20.4	10.3	40.3	35.6	24.1	26.2	12.6	23.2	2.6	4.7
d	9.6	2.3	31.9	16.4	12.4	11.7	36.5	54.1	9.6	15.5
f	2.1	1.6	10.1	5.6	6.3	2.8	48.7	54.3	32.8	35.6
g	.9	1.6	11.0	4.4	6.8	4.4	55.3	47.8	26.0	41.7
j	6.8	4.2	64.4	46.4	12.2	16.2	13.3	21.8	3.3	11.5
k	28.1	8.9	52.9	41.7	10.5	23.2	8.2	19.7	.2	6.6
l	19.7	7.5	45.4	37.9	11.7	14.8	19.9	30.9	3.3	8.9

SA Role

MODERN ← TRADITIONAL

| | Strongly Agree | | Agree | | Mixed Feelings | | Disagree | | Strongly Disagree | |
	1971	1975	1971	1975	1971	1975	1971	1975	1971	1975
c	8.7	7.7	26.0	46.1	23.7	24.6	38.2	19.4	3.5	2.1
e	6.3	8.0	37.9	61.4	22.2	16.9	30.4	12.6	3.0	1.2
h	10.5	12.4	54.6	67.7	20.6	11.9	12.6	8.0	1.6	.0
i	9.8	13.1	38.6	51.5	25.7	17.3	21.5	14.1	4.2	4.0

[a]*Total* in each row = 100%.
[b]See figure 1-1 for wording.

Table 1-5
Percentages of Wives by Their Responses to Role Items within Social Position of Husband, 1971 and 1975[a]
(n = 427)

	PHA Role									
	MODERN ←								TRADITIONAL	
	Strongly Agree		Agree		Mixed Feelings		Disagree		Strongly Disagree	
Items[b]	1971	1975	1971	1975	1971	1975	1971	1975	1971	1975
d	1.9	9.6	26.0	40.0	19.9	21.5	44.0	25.8	8.2	3.0
e	2.1	8.7	18.7	30.7	12.4	15.7	57.8	41.7	8.9	3.3
f	2.1	8.4	33.3	48.9	22.2	21.1	38.2	19.0	4.2	2.6
h	5.9	13.8	55.0	67.0	24.6	11.9	12.2	6.3	2.3	.9
i	1.9	10.1	37.5	56.0	29.7	17.1	28.3	15.2	2.6	1.6

	IE Role									
	MODERN ←								TRADITIONAL	
	Strongly Agree		Agree		Mixed Feelings		Disagree		Strongly Disagree	
	1971	1975	1971	1975	1971	1975	1971	1975	1971	1975
b	11.5	29.5	46.8	46.8	15.7	13.6	23.4	9.1	2.6	.9
c	14.1	33.7	64.9	57.8	10.5	6.3	10.3	1.6	.2	.0

	TH Role									
	TRADITIONAL								MODERN →	
	Strongly Agree		Agree		Mixed Feelings		Disagree		Strongly Disagree	
	1971	1975	1971	1975	1971	1975	1971	1975	1971	1975
a	7.3	8.0	28.1	25.8	17.6	20.4	42.6	40.7	4.4	5.2
g	31.6	30.0	53.4	43.1	8.0	11.2	6.3	13.1	.7	2.6

[a]*Total* in each row = 100%.
[b]See figure 1-1 for item wording.

modern. It is readily apparent that after four years the percentages of women found in the traditional categories have declined, whereas the percentages responding in the modern categories have increased.

The direction of changes in sex-role preferences is depicted by the arrows in tables 1-4, 1-5, and 1-6. Those who in 1971 had been strongly traditional had by 1975 moved into the less traditional, the ambivalent (mixed feelings), or the modern categories; the ambivalents had moved into the modern categories; and the 1971 moderns tended to remain stable or else had moved into the strongly modern categories. To be sure, some women shifted in the opposite, or traditional, direction as well, but they were a distinct minority.

Table 1-6
Percentages of Wives by Their Responses to Role Items within Social Position of Mother, 1971 and 1975[a]
(n = 427)

	RLM Role					
	TRADITIONAL					MODERN
	Yes		Uncertain		No	
Items[b]	1971	1975	1971	1975	1971	1975
a	84.8	83.6	4.7	4.0	10.5	12.4
b	78.0	70.3	3.0	3.7	19.0	26.0

	TM Role					
	MODERN					TRADITIONAL
	Yes		Uncertain		No	
	1971	1975	1971	1975	1971	1975
c	52.5	67.9	2.5	6.1	45.0	26.0
d	56.0	67.4	4.7	4.2	39.3	28.3
e	29.0	46.8	2.4	4.4	68.6	48.7
f	35.4	48.9	2.3	7.1	62.3	44.0
g	26.2	36.3	3.5	11.2	70.3	52.5

[a]*Total* in each row = 100%.
[b]See figure 1-1 for item wording.

The predominant mood displayed by these quantitative data is captured by this verbatim qualitative response from one woman:

I think I would like him to have more . . . understanding towards things I feel strongly about. . . . I cannot be the way I was ten years ago. I'm not a child any more and he can't understand some of the things I do. We're going through a difficult time right now. . . . Basically I have to be an individual, a person as well as his wife. I have to be more than someone to clean house and take care of the house. I want to maybe go to college. I want to walk *with* him not *behind* him. He is trying to understand. He is backtracking and trying very hard to understand. I don't think I can be the person I was eleven years ago. It drives me crazy to just sit home. We're trying to understand each other. I don't want to destroy his ego so I have to handle this with grace. The problem is I am no longer completely dependent on him and he can't seem to understand this. Each year I am becoming a little more independent and he has a hard time understanding this. If he would have a little more patience and understanding of me, and accept the fact that I have changed in eleven years, you know, he might realize that he might be like me, because after all he's a changed person but doesn't see himself as changed—he only sees me as changed and he can't understand why. If he would be a little patient with me and try to understand me things would be so great. After all, what he doesn't understand is that with raising four children I have to change—I can't remain the same. Because this is a changing world with different attitudes and I have to lead a different life than I did before I was married or before I had children. Like I said before I want to walk with him and not behind him. I guess that's it but it sure would be nice if we could iron this out.

Viewed, therefore, from the perspective of the individual items in tables 1-4, 1-5, and 1-6, as well as from the composite mean scores in table 1-2, it seems that these respondents fit the pattern found by the studies cited earlier. These women are part of what appears to be a general trend in American (and Western) society toward more egalitarian (less traditional) definitions of gender roles.

The 1975 reinterview had a further major purpose: to probe in considerable depth the meanings of women's work, its consequences, and how women negotiate and conflict in marriage. Those issues are the substance of the next four chapters.

Summary

The central theme of this book is the analysis of three aspects of marital/familial change using an eclectic reward/cost approach. The notion of preferences for certain valued goals is central to such an approach, and it is argued that several highly interrelated sex-role dimensions may be used as indicators of the degree to which women prefer continued gender differentiation or gender interchangeability. Evidence is presented showing shifts over time by women (and to a lesser extent by men) in the direction of stronger preferences for greater interchangeability.

Thus, at the core of the issue of family change in general is variation in degree of preferred differentiation as opposed to preferred interchangeability. More specifically, the argument of the following chapters is that that sort of variation is related to and helps account for changes in the *meanings* and *consequences* of women's work, as well as in the ways in which they negotiate with their husbands.

Notes

1. Use of this approach in no way excludes analyses at the macro level.

2. During the summer of 1975, National Analysts (NA) undertook to locate and reinterview younger white wives interviewed four years previously (File, 1975). The names and 1971 addresses of the total eligible 590 women were made available to NA. At the time of the 1971 survey there were no plans to reinterview these women; hence, none of the steps were taken that are usually

done in panel designs to enhance locatability of younger respondents, who tend to be exceedingly geographically mobile. "Approximately half of the respondents who were ultimately interviewed had moved at least once from their 1971 addresses" (File, 1975:2). For example, names and 1971 addresses were not obtained of relatives and neighbors who might have been able to keep track of them during the interval. In spite of that considerable initial handicap, NA was able to locate and interview 427, or 72.4 percent, of the original respondents. Of that number, 66 had moved out of the original 1971 ten-city SMSAs to other parts of the country. These women were among those successfully traced and interviewed. An additional 49 women were located but not interviewed. Three of these were deceased and 46 were refusals. That last figure is 9.7 percent of all respondents living and contacted. NA reports that "a sizable proportion of refusals were due to the intercession of the husband. In a number of cases, husbands refused permission for our interviewers even to talk to the respondent, much less conduct the interviews. In such circumstances, interviewers attempted direct contact with the respondent when the husband was unlikely to be home. A few interviews were thereby obtained, with the woman consenting in defiance of her husband's desires" (File 1975:5). A total of 114 respondents (19.3 percent of the original sample) could not be located for reinterview even though "an average of four different tracing attempts were made in an effort to locate each of these respondents" (p. 7). Approximately half of these were traced through several addresses and often into other states, but at a certain point there was no longer any additional information to permit NA to continue the search. Among the remainder, usually from larger cities, "very little information was ever obtained" (p. 7). Though neighbors, post offices, schools, other community sources, and so on, were utilized exhaustively, no trace of these persons could be found.

This report, therefore, is based on those 427 women who were interviewed in 1971 and again in 1975. But what about those not reinterviewed? Are they in any way systematically different from those who were? For instance, are the nonlocatables the most poorly educated, or the very best educated? Most important, how would any differences that exist bias the analyses we hope to do in following chapters? To try to answer those questions as fully as possible, table 1-7 compares women located in 1975 with nonlocatables. The data, of course, are based on their 1971 responses.

Let us first examine those variables for which no significant differences appear. These include husbands' age, education, job status, and income. Also, no significant differences emerge for age at marriage, wives' education, fathers' job status, and parents' education. The same conclusion applies to number of children desired, number of months between marriage and first child, marital satisfactions, economic satisfactions, five dimensions of wife and husband gender-role modernity, and the two self-concept dimensions. There are also no significant differences in the proportion of their married lives spent in the labor force, in the number of those who worked full time prior to marriage, in the number employed full time in 1971, or in their religious preferences.

Table 1-7

Comparisons over Key Variables between 1971 Respondents Located in 1975 and Those Not Located

(Mean Scores; 1971 values)

	Locatables	*Nonlocatables*
Wife's age	24.00	23.40*
Family size	1.50	1.25*
Births intended	2.70	2.47*
RLM role[a]	1.67	1.52*
TM role[a]	2.93	2.70*
Wife's education	12.10	12.20**
Husband's education	12.60	12.70
Father's job status (wife)	60.00	61.70
Father's education (wife)	10.40	10.60
Mother's education (wife)	10.70	10.80
Age at marriage	19.40	19.60
Births desired	2.80	2.70
TW role[a]	18.10	17.40
SA role[b]	9.00	8.90
PHA role[b]	9.65	9.80
TH role[a]	5.00	4.91
IE role[b]	5.20	5.00
Wife-abilities (AE)[a]	5.60	5.60
Instrumental self-concept[a]	2.60	2.70
Expressive self-concept[a]	3.50	3.50
Empathy satisfaction[a]	1.00	1.00
Economic satisfaction[a]	1.30	1.30
Father's job status (husband)	57.70	57.50
Husband's age	26.20	26.10
Husband's job status	63.40	62.70
Husband's income[c]	8.60	8.40
Months until first child	20.30	21.00
Proportion of time in labor force	.34	.34
Percentage who:**		
Worked prior to marriage	69	68
Worked full time	40	44
Non-Catholic	62	67
Had 1970 income	58	57
(n)	(427)	(164)

*Significant at .05.

**None of the following differences significant.

[a]Low score = greater modernity or more positive perception.

[b]High score = greater modernity.

[c]In thousands of dollars.

Nevertheless, although these variables do not differ significantly, there is some consistency that may be worth noting. For instance, nonlocatables have slightly more education, and so do their husbands. Their parents ranked somewhat higher in status, their birth desires were slightly lower, and their preferences for gender-role egalitarianism were somewhat stronger. These observations would mean nothing were it not for five additional variables on which there are significant differences. The nonlocatables were significantly younger, they intended to have and actually had fewer children, and they were more modern or egalitarian on both aspects of the mother position.

In sum, if forced to make a judgment based on these data, one might say that in some respects the nonlocatables include some of the women who would be most useful to the study's objectives.

In any case, whatever bias might exist among the locatables, it does not appear to be very large or overwhelming. More important, given the direction of the bias, any evidence that emerges in the following chapters of significant relationships in the expected directions becomes that much more impressive. That is, if gender (sex) roles are related to employment and conflict behaviors in significant ways among the locatables, then one can assume that the relationships would have been even stronger had we been able to include the nonlocatables as well.

3. For example, among women who were working at both the 1971 and 1975 interview points, the sex-role beta weight was .23, stronger than any other predictor variable in the equation (see Scanzoni, 1979a).

4. Reliability coefficients (ALPHAS) TW 71 = .74, SA 71 = .56, TW 75 = .81, SA 75 = .63.

5. ALPHAS: PHA 71 = .62, IE 71 = .68, TH 71 = .20, PHA 75 = .68, IE 75 = .74, TH 75 = .38.

6. ALPHAS: RLM 71 = .62, TM 71 = .47, RLM 75 = .65, TM 75 = .63.

2 Women and the Meaning of Work

Introduction

If work (paid employment) has the same meaning or significance to all women (namely, that it is an option which is exercised to help out the family primarily when it experiences periodic financial stress), and if it appears that that meaning has been constant for many decades and will probably remain so, then we may conclude that assertions by the media or social scientists of fundamental changes in marital structure simply due to increased labor-force participation would be premature. Since the idea of work as option is intrinsic to long-standing marriage patterns (Spiegel, 1957), more people exercising that option does not by itself indicate basic structural change.

The assertion of work-related change in those long-standing marriage patterns could be justified if it could be shown that some women are moving away from defining work merely as an option, that is, that there is variation among women in the images they hold of paid employment. This is precisely the theme of this chapter. We shall see that there is indeed heterogeneity in the ways women view labor-force participation. Some continue to lean more toward the idea of work as an option; others tend to edge away from that long-standing meaning of work, and toward something quite different.

Questions as to work's meanings are central to any attempt to grasp and understand contemporary marital change. The demographic shifts reported in chapter 1 are merely symptomatic of the state of affairs of these kinds of issues. To overlook these microlevel questions in trying to devise social policies, educational programs, or therapy strategies is to fail to take cognizance of the shifting assumptions on which one may be building.

The emphasis in this chapter fits under the rubric of purposive action or reward-cost theory in that we want to test the proposition that women who are more sex-role egalitarian are more likely to be altering their definitions of work. The preferences of such women, in general, lean in a more individualistic direction; that is, they want higher levels of occupational benefits and fewer household encumbrances that undercut those individualistic pursuits. Since chapter 1 supplied evidence of sex-role changes in general, it follows that those changes should be linked at a more specific level to how work is viewed. Therefore, my basic hypothesis throughout this chapter is that sex-role traditionalism is related to, and presumably influences, a definition of work as merely an option to be exercised as circumstances demand. Conversely, sex-role modernity influences women to conceive of work primarily as what I describe as a right. Such a definition is conveyed through the following statement from a media discussion of how some employed women deal with the demands and expectations of the Christmas holiday season:

> First, know exactly what your work means to you. Not one of these women apologizes to her family for working. For them, work is a prime source of satisfaction, which they're not about to sacrifice to the rigors of a holiday. (Lamb, 1977:47)

It goes without saying that such an outlook on work stands in sharp contrast to the idea that it is merely an emergency option exercised to meet family needs.

Some years ago Noble (1966) characterized the black woman as a "working citizen." She was attempting to show that up through the early sixties most white women exhibited the kind of work discontinuity described in chapter 1. Working was an option to be exercised when it did not interfere with interests of husband and children. In contrast, ever since emancipation, women within black society have been forced to seek paid employment because of economic discrimination against black men. Therefore, female employment has become much more institutionalized or normative among blacks (Scanzoni, 1977:228-32; 1975b).

One result of that pattern is that working has become less of an option and more of a right for many black women. *Option* is defined as permissible behavior; but the behavior is limited or constrained by certain contingencies such as the interests of husband and children. *Right* is defined as behavior that is more or less inherent in a particular role. Constraints are never absent but they are relatively minimal. With an option the burden rests with actors to demonstrate that it is legitimate for them to act, for example, during the sixties, a mother of preschoolers who worked. With a right the burden rests with others to try to prevent the actor's purposes. Former Attorney General Ramsey Clark said, "a right is not what someone gives you; it's what no one can take from you." An adult has the right to vote; a police officer the right to brandish weapons; a principal the right to expel students; the black married woman the right to work.

At present, some younger white women are coming to define work in the way that has characterized black women for some time. The question is: What are the conditions under which work takes on such great importance to women that they cease defining it as an option and begin seeing it as a right?

I propose that there are at least seven conditions or characteristics that can be used to assess or indicate the extent to which some women view working as more or less a right or an option: (1) intangible resources, (2) occupational achievement orientations, (3) career orientations, (4) occupational satisfactions, (5) relative import of wife's vis-à-vis husband's occupation, (6) husband's occupational mobility in the interests of wife's occupation, and (7) relative import of wife's job vis-à-vis contraints of children. Each of these seven dimensions may be thought of as a continuum. Women can be found at the high or low points on each one or somewhere in between. My argument will be that women who rank toward the "high" end of the continuum tend to view work as a right, whereas those who rank toward the "low" end are more likely to view it as an option.

Intangible Resources

The first of the seven indicators of the meaning that women attach to work is intangible resources. Emerson observed that rewards are not necessarily synonymous with resources (1976:247-248). Resources are elements that actors or groups may use to gain certain goals in social situations. A child may receive candy from another child in exchange for assistance and both of them consider the candy a great reward. If the candy is not eaten, the child may then use it the next day as a resource to get something he or she wants from a third child. But should the child use the candy to seek favored treatment from the teacher, it is almost certain to be worthless. Since it is not a valued reward to the teacher, it is not a resource to the child in that situation.

Money is a universal tangible resource in modern society and women can use it to bargain for desired goals within marriage and the family. If they are sufficient, alternative economic resources permit women to dissolve the association and support themselves. Tangible resources also permit married women to achieve desired objectives outside the family. But, as noted in chapter 1, all resources are not tangible. A skill is not thought of as tangible. But if A has it and B needs it applied to something, then A can get a reward (tangible or intangible) from B for applying it. That skill has clearly been a resource.

Therefore, while devising questions to probe the meaning of work, it was thought to be incumbent that we get some indication of the intangible resources these wives felt they possessed.

> I am going to read some different kinds of abilities which some women have. Compared to most women of your age how would you say you compare, when it comes to: (*Here, read items in figure 2-1*). Would you say: better or more than most; better or more than some; about the same; not as good; or as much as most?

The results were factor-analyzed, and the dimensions or resource clusters that emerged appear in figure 2-1.[1]

The *external*-resource dimension is defined as "skills or capabilities that generate goal attainment in systems outside the family—especially the occupational system." The *internal* resource dimension is defined as "skills or capabilities that generate goal attainment within the family." A third resource

External

b. Entertaining, being a good hostess.

e. Ability to organize activities outside the family.

f. Natural intelligence

g. Ability to handle a number of responsibilities outside the family.

i. Ability to be a leader in places outside the family.

n. Ability to solve problems of people outside your family.

o. Ability to earn a good living on your own.

p. Ambitious to have a life of your own.

q. Aggressive to get what you want out of life.

r. Confidence to do things right outside your family.

Internal

h. Ability to solve problems you have with your husband.

k. Ability to get what is right and fair from your husband.

t. Ability to help your husband solve problems he has at work.

u. Ability to keep up with your husband or other men sexually.

Appreciation

l. Ability to be appreciated by an employer.

m. Ability to be appreciated by friends at work.

Figure 2-1. Dimensions of Intangible Resources Possessed by Women, 1975

dimension appears very infrequently throughout the pages that follow, but nonetheless merits brief consideration. *Appreciation* is "the degree of perceived evaluation or *esteem* in which actors are held by significant others in the world of work." Presumably, that esteem provides a certain degree of bargaining leverage.

But not all women have equal amounts of these intangible resources (any more than they have equal levels of tangible resources), and the question becomes *why*. What accounts for differences among women in this regard—why do some have more intangible resources than others? Among wives who worked at the 1975 interview, three clusters of variables provide at least a partial response.

First is the social class background from which these women came. The more education each of their parents had, and the higher their father's job status, the more external resources the daughters possessed.[2] Second, their own education was positively related to external resources.[3] Finally, their own sex roles were also positively associated.[4] Among nonworkers, only their education and sex roles were related to external resources.[5]

Elsewhere (Scanzoni, 1975b) I reported that better-educated parents transmit more modern sex-role preferences to their daughters. In addition, it turns out that better-educated, higher-status parents pass on skills and capabilities that enable their daughters to realize the attainment of those preferences. They also, of course, encourage their daughters to stay in school longer.[6] Thus from all three perspectives it is clear that coming from a more advantaged background makes a substantial difference. Such women learn to prefer individualistic goals or rewards; they also learn to develop the means (intangible resources) to attain the goals; and they gain more of the tangible resources (education) that make goal attainment that much more possible. It may be said that through the years of adolescence and early marriage, sex roles, external resources, and education become intrinsically interlocked and mutually reinforcing. While sex (or gender) roles establish preferences, the two remaining elements increase the likelihood of their realization, which reinforces the preferences, which stimulates further resource development, and so the cycle continues. For instance, sex-role egalitarianism may develop resources by encouraging women to place themselves in situations (more schooling, more demanding occupations) where they must test themselves to see how many external resources they actually have. This often results in discovery of a range and depth of resources of which they had no idea.

Why nonworkers reveal no link between external resources and social-class background is not certain. Table 2-1 shows that nonworkers score significantly lower on this resource than workers. It would appear that some parents do not

Table 2-1
Differences between Working and Nonworking Wives Over Selected Key Variables
(mean scores)

	Worked at 1975 Interview	Not Working at 1975 Interview	Significance Level
Education (years)	12.2	11.9	.09
Husband's education (years)	12.8	12.5	.19
TW 1971[a]	17.5	18.7	.01
TM 1971[a]	2.8	3.1	.03
TW 1975[a]	13.6	15.2	.00
SA 1975[b]	10.9	10.0	.00
PHA 1975[b]	12.6	11.8	.02
IE 1975[b]	6.3	6.1	.35
TH 1975[c]	4.6	4.9	.07
RLM 1975[c]	1.5	1.6	.22
TM 1975[c]	2.0	2.3	.06
Number of children 1975	1.7	2.3	.00
Births intended 1975	2.2	2.6	.00
Husband job status 1975[c]	44.7	41.3	.16
Husband income 1975[d]	12.6	13.9	.02
External resources	15.7	12.3	.00
Internal resources	6.9	6.5	.12
Appreciation resources	3.7	3.1	.00
Continuity (months)	48.9	11.0	.00
Age of last child (years)	7.1	4.0	.00

[a]Lower score = stronger preferences for gender egalitarianism.

[b]Higher score = stronger preferences for gender egalitarianism.

[c]Duncan Socioeconomic Index.

[d]In thousands of dollars.

train their daughters very strongly in the development of external resources. Consequently, such women are less likely to have confidence that they can "make it" in the world of work; and therefore they are apparently less likely to seek employment at any given point during their early marriage.

Parenthetically, this observed difference between workers and nonworkers in background socialization is one reason why, in this and in the following chapters, I have separated working from nonworking wives. As I first discovered when analyzing their 1971 responses (Scanzoni, 1975b), the two categories of women live in very different social situations. The kinds of issues I want to explore would be blurred and could not be researched validly by looking at the two kinds of women together. While that conclusion was true when investigating their 1971 fertility patterns, it is doubly true for questions of work meanings, work consequences, and conflict processes. Indeed, the many contrasts between the two categories revealed in these chapters contribute a great deal to our understanding of the differing life situations of workers and nonworkers.

Table 2-1, for instance, shows that (compared with nonworkers) workers tend to be somewhat better-educated, more sex-role egalitarian, to intend to have and actually have fewer children, to have an older last child, and to have had much more work continuity. Furthermore, even if one wanted to look at the two categories together, there are certain vital questions explored in this and especially in the next chapter that cannot simply be put to nonworkers. These include, for example, occupational-achievement orientations (table 2-2) which are based on the premise that the respondent actually currently holds an occupation.

Internal and Appreciation Resources

Nevertheless, both sets of women show no connections between the two remaining types of intangible resources described earlier (figure 2-1) and factors such as education, sex roles, or class background. However, among workers and nonworkers alike, external resources are correlated to internal resources (figure 2-1).[7] Since internal resources bear no connection to class background, it seems that external resources exercise more prior and prime influence over internal resources than the other way around. Obviously, over time, there are mutual feedback effects. But it can be assumed that at the outset of marriage, women who have learned to be more goal-effective in the larger society carry this over into the family. Conversely, women with fewer external resources seem less likely to develop internal resources.

Similarly, the possession of external skills and capabilities seems to stimulate the development of appreciation-type resources as well (figure 2-1).[8] The capability to function well in the world of work apparently does tend to enhance one's value or esteem in the eyes of significant others at work.

Resources and the Right to Work

Recall that *right* is defined as an actor's institutionalized or accepted behavior that others can try to contravene with only the greatest of effort—perhaps often conflict. Possession of intangible resources may be taken as one indicator of the degree to which women are likely to define working as a right, as opposed to an option. Women who do not possess these external resources are presumably less able to do well in the occupational sector. Fewer internal resources make them less able to negotiate their husbands into household arrangements that would facilitate their employment. Therefore, since the work world is less rewarding and the domestic scene more punishing (should they try to work); there is less reason to conceive of work as a right. It is sufficient for them that work be an option. In contrast, high-resource women are more likely to reason, "Since I can do it so well, why shouldn't I?" In other words, the more rewarding and less costly an activity is (that is, more profitable) the more likely persons are to regard it as their right. If the activity is only marginally worthwhile, persons are likely to view it with greater indifference, and regard it as an option.

Added to this picture is the connection between resources and egalitarianism. Low-resource women hold fewer gender-related preferences which make it urgent to define work as their right. In contrast, high-resource women do hold preferences that seem to make it essential to define work as more than a mere option. Therefore, on the one side, resources are an indicator of the meaning of work because resources generate benefits or profit. What is highly profitable is more likely to be defined as a valued right. What is less profitable is not. On the other side is the linkage between egalitarianism and resources. Women who prefer modern-type gratifications are more likely to define working as a right and to have more resources.

Achievement and Career Orientations

But having intangible resources is no guarantee that women are going to be able to achieve as fully as men in the occupational sector. Pervasive discrimination and traditional socialization patterns are the root causes of this divergence. Since up until recently it was rare to investigate the achievements of women, social scientists did not take women's employment seriously. It was thought of merely as an option, not a right, and simply did not generate much attention.

Items such as those displayed in figure 2-2 were applied chiefly to men, although Turner used them for both sexes (1964). But if increasing numbers of married women are becoming "consistent workers" (compare chapter 1; also F.D. Blau, 1975; Maret-Havens, 1977; Scanzoni, 1979b) then it becomes just as significant to assess women's achievement orientations as it does to assess those of males. Indeed, it can be argued that high achievement orientations are a

Current Evaluation

Here are a series of numbers which describe how people are doing in their job or occupation. As you can see they go from "Not doing as well as most people," to "Doing much better than everyone else." Which number describes *where you stand* right now?

1. Not doing as well as most people.
2. Doing as well as most people.
3. Doing a little better than most people.
4. Doing much better than most people.
5. One of the top persons in your job or occupation.
6. Doing better than everyone else.

Current Aspirations

If you had a choice, which of the six statements *best* describes where you *would like to be* right now?

      1 2 3 4 5 6

Future Aspirations

Which of the six statements best describes where you *hope* to be someday?

      1 2 3 4 5 6

Expectations

Realistically, do you think the chances that you will reach where you hope to be someday are good, fair, or poor?

Figure 2-2. Achievement Orientations that Wives hold for Themselves and for Husbands (Wording slightly altered when applied to men)

second indicator of work as a right. Conversely, women who hold lower orientations may be said to think of it more as an option.

Therefore, the questions in figure 2-2 were asked of working wives about themselves and separately regarding their husbands. Nonworkers were queried solely in regard to husbands. The top rows of table 2-2 compare workers and nonworkers on how they feel about their husbands' achievement behaviors.

No significant differences emerge. Both sets of wives evaluate their husbands' current occupational performance at similar levels. Moreover, their aspirations, both present and future, for higher performance levels by their husbands are also at comparable levels. Finally, the wives' expectation *levels* of husbands actually attaining their (wives') stated aspirations do not differ. In short, working does not significantly alter wives' orientations regarding husbands' achievements. Workers, for instance, are not disappointed by their husbands' performances and thereby motivated to work in order to compensate.

The middle rows of table 2-2 compare the achievement orientations that all working wives hold for themselves with those they hold for their husbands. The

Table 2-2
Achievement Orientations Held by Wives for Husbands and Themselves

	Current Evaluations	Current Aspirations	Future Aspirations	Expectations
Orientations for Husbands				
1975 Workers (*n* = 162)	3.19	4.35	4.81	2.68
	*	*	*	*
1975 Nonworkers (*n* = 233)	3.16	4.19	4.82	2.66
1975 Workers (n = 162)				
Orientation for husbands	3.19	4.35	4.81	2.68
	**	**	**	*
Orientation for themselves	2.80	4.07	4.42	2.65
1975 Full-time Workers (n = 110)				
Orientations for husbands	3.03	4.36	4.80	2.65
	*	*	**	*
Orientation for themselves	2.90	4.24	4.55	2.67

*Not significant.
**Significant at .01 or beyond.

question is: Are workers as achievement-oriented for themselves as they are for their husbands? These data suggest that they are not. Strong significant differences emerge on three dimensions. Workers rank themselves lower than they rank their husbands on evaluations of current occupational attainments, as well as on aspirations for current and future performances. Nevertheless, they do not rank themselves significantly different than they rank their husbands as to expectations that aspirations for the future will actually be attained.

In other words, though they may rank husbands' actual performance as higher, and hold higher aspirations for their husbands than they do for themselves, that divergence fails to hold regarding expectations. Once working women set their own aspirations, they expect that they will achieve them as strongly as they expect their husbands to achieve the goals set for them.

The findings that workers hold lower achievement orientations for themselves than for their husbands, reflect a number of phenomena including traditional gender socialization, sex discrimination, and less work continuity (compare table 1-1). Part-time work might be another factor that is associated with achievement orientations. Therefore, a more valid comparison of those orientations might be obtained from full-time women workers as in the bottom rows of table 2-2. No significant differences occur between the evaluations, current aspirations, and expectations that full-time workers hold for themselves and for their husbands.

Thus achievement orientations for self and spouse are much more congruent among women who probably have been more work-consistent, and currently are as much involved in the labor force as their husbands. It is only on future aspirations that they continue to rank themselves below their husbands, and that may very well reflect less continuity (months in the labor force) throughout the course of their married lives. That is, if they had been as work-active as their husbands, they may have been able to develop enough confidence to hold the same kinds of long-term future aspirations for themselves as they hold for their husbands. In the past, it is likely that women workers (even full-time) ranked themselves even further behind their husbands in all types of achievement orientations than they do at present. The future should see a continued lessening of those differences, including their aspirations for long-range attainments.

One factor that may have impeded women's long-range occupational plans in the past was the contingency of children. "If a child should happen to come along" they might have reasoned, "I would then be forced to interrupt my work." Thus it was (and is) difficult for a woman to make long-range occupational plans. But evidence elsewhere (Scanzoni, 1975b) and later in this chapter suggests that children may exercise somewhat less constraint on women's employment than once they did. In support of that notion, recent government data reveal that one of the fastest growing categories of women currently entering the labor force are those with preschool children (Hayghe, 1975). Formerly such women were the least likely to have been employed.

Current Occupational Evaluations

Having said the foregoing, it is instructive to examine the section of table 2-3 that accounts for working wives' current job performance.[9] The higher they rank their husbands on the six levels in figure 2-2, the higher they rank themselves. The explanation for this connection can be traced in part to the common location of husbands and wives in the educational structure, based on the correlation (.59) between their education levels. Husbands' own education, job status, and income are the strongest determinants of women's evaluations of their husbands' current performance. Not surprisingly, women married to higher-status men are more likely to evaluate their husbands' job performance more positively.

Concomitantly, note that the second strongest influence on workers' self-evaluations is their own 1974 income. As reported elsewhere (Scanzoni, 1979a) the more sex-role-modern women were in 1971, the more money they earned by 1974.[10] Recall that egalitarian or modern sex-role preferences are also strongly correlated with education. Thus, better-educated, sex-role-modern women earned more dollars in 1974, and that outcome leads them to evaluate

Table 2-3
Influences on Achievement Orientations, Occupational Definitions, and
Job Satisfaction by Employment Status

Workers (n = 162)						
Current Evaluations				*Current Aspirations*		
	beta	*r*			*beta*	*r*
Evaluation of husband	.35	.38		Current evaluations	.42	.51
1974 income	.26	.34		External resource	.19	.38
Appreciation	.20	.31		1975 SA modernity	.15	.29
Career	.18	.32				
MR = .58, R² = .34				*MR = .57, R² = .33*		
Future Aspirations				*Expectations*		
	beta	*r*			*beta*	*r*
Current aspirations	.69	.75		Career definition	.21	.23
Worked 1971	.12	.24		Future aspirations	−.23	−.14
Job status	.06*	.23		External resource	.16	.16
1975 SA modernity	.06*	.29				
External resource	.03*	.33				
MR = .77, R² = .59				*MR = .32, R² = .11*		
Career Definition				*Career Preferred*		
	beta	*r*			*beta*	*r*
Work for enjoyment	.33	.43		External resource	.37	.51
1975 TW modernity	.20	.40		1975 TW modernity	.28	.46
External resource	.19	.39		Work for enjoyment	.15	.29
Job status	.17	.30				
MR = .59, R² = .35				*MR = .60, R² = .36*		

Occupational Satisfaction		
	beta	*r*
Career definition	.23	.31
Work for enjoyment	.15	.28
1971 Economic satisfaction	.11*	.18
MR = .36, R² = .13		

Nonworkers (n = 233)		
Career Preferred		
	beta	*r*
1971 PHA modernity	.16	.16
Education	.11	.20
Catholic	.14	.14
Evaluation of husband	.12	.20
Husband job status	.10*	.19
MR = .33, R² = .11		

All betas significant at .05, unless starred.

their own 1975 job performance more positively. These tangible benefits become a prime means to assess their own overall job performance, just as their husbands' tangible outputs influence them in assessing their husbands' performance. Hence, among wives who are both egalitarian and economically advantaged, certain kinds of influence are common both to their evaluations of their husbands and of themselves.

At the same time, it is possible to suggest an additional and related reason why wives' own evaluations of themselves are predicted by their evaluations of their husbands. Were husbands asked to evaluate the occupational performance of their working wives, it is unlikely that many would rank their wives higher than they rank themselves. In part that is because wives generally tend to earn less than husbands. But it might also reflect a sense of rivalry and unwillingness to acknowledge that their wives are actually outperforming them.

Concomitantly, working wives also may sense some degree of (presumably cordial) rivalry. Hence, relative to where they rank their husbands' performance, they rank themselves behind them, but not too far behind (table 2-2). And, of course, as table 2-2 shows, full-time workers (68 percent of the employed) do not rank themselves significantly behind their husbands at all.

Workers may not wish to acknowledge that their husbands are "outperforming" them by too great a distance. Instead they prefer to evaluate their two performances as relatively comparable. In any case, this kind of issue would seem to be pertinent to explore in future investigations of patterns and processes within working-wife households, especially if younger women become increasingly achievement-oriented and thus the potential for relative spouse comparisons enlarges.

This last point is underscored in view of the two remaining predictors of wives' performance. The first of these—appreciation—suggests that having the ability to be esteemed or valued by peers and superiors is a resource in terms of three goals such as job retention, promotion, and wage increments. Being valued implies that they are able to provide work peers with assistance in the senses so frequently discussed by Homans (1974) and P.M. Blau (1964). It also means they are able to accomplish tasks set for them by superiors. Women who possess that resource are therefore more likely to gain the above three goals, and that is precisely what the data indicate. The greater the appreciation, the higher their evaluation of current job performance.

Work as Career

The fourth variable in the first section of table 2-3 that predicts job evaluation centers around whether respondents themselves label their own occupations as jobs or careers. The term *career* as applied to women's employment has been used in several studies (Fogarty et al., 1971; Parnes and Nestle, 1975; Burke and

Weir, 1976). However, it is not always clear that the term *career* has been defined in rigorous fashion or, more importantly, that it has meant the same thing to respondents as it does to researchers.

To try to minimize those sorts of semantic problems, the terms *career* and *job* were explicitly defined. *Career* was defined for the respondent as "something where people work a lot of extra hours without extra pay. They are sometimes away from home evenings or weekends but it gives them a lot of satisfaction in addition to money." The respondent was also told that "some people think of their work as 'just a job.' That is, something where they work a set number of hours and then go home and forget it." Based on these contrasting images, it is not surprising that "career women" should see themselves as doing better occupationally than "job holders." The additional time and energy that they are willing to devote to their occupations are likely to produce outcomes in terms of salary and position that enable them to evaluate their job situation as highly as they do.

As might be expected, sex-role preferences exercise considerable direct and indirect influence on "career definition" as indicated in row 3 of table 2-3. For example, the strongest predictor of career orientation is job motivation: wives who state they are motivated to work more for "enjoyment" than for "money" are more likely to define their work as a career instead of a job. But wives who are more gender-role egalitarian are also more likely to work because they enjoy it.[11] Consequently, gender-modern wives who enjoy work are also more likely to see it as a career since they are willing to labor additional hours without extra pay and forego certain evenings and weekends. In turn, that willingness for extra efforts accounts for their current positive occupational evaluations.

Sex-role preferences are also a direct positive predictor of a career orientation.[12] Thus, egalitarianism not only affects career orientations via work motivation, it has its own direct impact—egalitarian wives are more likely to be career-oriented. Similarly, egalitarian wives possess more external resources; the more resources possessed, the more likely women are to define themselves as holding a career. Having more intangible resources enables women to meet the additional, more stringent demands imposed by careers as opposed to jobs.

Finally, holding a higher status, more prestigious occupation also predicts a career orientation.[13] Women who receive more tangible and intangible benefits are more likely to think of their work as a career, which is likely to lead to still greater levels of both types of benefits. As was true with 1974 income, the 1975 job status of these wives was influenced positively by 1971 sex-role preferences (Scanzoni, 1979a).[14] In short, desires for gender equality and interchangeability, as indicated by sex-role preferences, gradually emerge as a key element among the interlocking web of factors analyzed in table 2-3.

Recall that earlier I listed career orientation as the third indicator of work meaning, the second being occupational achievement orientations. Although the rationale for using career orientation in that fashion should by now be somewhat apparent, I shall delay further elaboration of that rationale until we complete our consideration of the remaining achievement dimensions.

Occupational Aspirations

Current Aspirations. This section of table 2-3 accounts for the present aspirations of these wives. At which of the six points in figure 2-2 would they like to be right now? The strongest predictor is the performance level at which they actually are; the higher they are, the higher they would like to be. Thus, their aspirations are the outcome of the same chain of influences that has already affected their current evaluations.

That conclusion is supported by the two remaining positive influences on aspirations. One is their level of external resources. Wives who believe that they have the resources necessary to achieve at higher levels are more likely to want to actually be at those levels.

Second, to be strongly egalitarian on the self-actualization (SA) sex-role dimension is also to aspire to higher occupational performance. Wives who prefer the individualistic benefits inherent in more modern gender-role preferences are therefore likely to be more achievement-oriented. Gender preferences prescribe domains of costs and rewards, rights and obligations. Women who hold more egalitarian preferences are prescribing for themselves that the rights and rewards (as well as the costs and obligations) of greater occupational achievements are legitimate goals for them to pursue.

Future Aspirations. As might be expected from the correlation with current aspirations, that variable is by far the strongest influence on future aspirations. However, in spite of that relationship, women's future aspirations are significantly higher than their current aspirations.[15] Thus, current evaluations influence current aspirations, which strongly affect aspirations for the future.

And because of the presence of current aspirations, the table shows that job status, sex-role modernity and external resources do not have much direct impact on future aspirations. Nevertheless, it is clear that women who aspire to higher future job performance also rank higher on all three elements.

Importantly, one variable does directly influence future aspirations. Current workers who also worked at the time of the 1971 interview tended to aspire to higher future achievement aspirations than those who did not. Thus women who worked at point 1 in time, and are again working at point 2, are the ones most likely to aspire to greater achievement levels at point 3 sometime in the future. Their consistency of effort leads them to want to continue working, and also to perform at higher levels than women who have not demonstrated as much consistency as they have.

Occupational Expectations

Finally, the related section of table 2-3 shows that wives who define their occupations as a career are more likely to expect to actually attain their future aspirations than wives who define them as jobs. Concomitantly, wives who possess more external resources are also more optimistic about the future—they are more confident that they in fact have the capabilities to attain the performance level to which they aspire. Both these predictor variables were theoretically foreseen, since both have been affected by sex-role preferences. Women who have become more egalitarian develop more external resources, and they also develop stronger career orientations. In turn, they are more likely to hold stronger achievement expectations.

The Aspirations-Expectations Paradox. But what was unforeseen is the negative influence of the future-aspirations variable: the higher their achievement aspirations, the lower their expectations that they will ever realize them. Merton (1957) has indicated that the gap between aspirations (what persons would like to have) and expectations (what persons actually expect to get) is highly significant, both theoretically and policy-wise. Women or men may aspire to very high achievement levels but actually expect very modest ones, and the disparity may result in frustration which, according to Merton, could have negative consequences both for the larger society and the persons involved.

What the nature of any such negative consequences might be for women, their husbands or children, or their own job performance is not apparent at this time. But clearly such matters deserve considerable research. For what appears to be operating among working women are two sets of related, but ultimately paradoxical, forces. On the one side are those factors that contribute towards greater attainments and increasingly higher aspirations for individualistic rewards. Some of these kinds of factors do in turn have a direct positive impact on actual expectations, as the table reveals.

But on the other side, as those aspirations grow increasingly greater, they reduce women's expectations of ever actually gaining them. This paradoxical phenomenon is restricted to their own life situations because there are positive correlations between the aspirations and expectations they hold for their husbands.

The paradox may be due to several factors, one of which is job discrimination. They may believe that the higher the performance level to which they aspire, the more difficult it becomes to avoid sex-based discrimination in salary and opportunities for promotion. Another related factor may be relatively less continuity in the past; less experience and lack of seniority may be seen as a handicap to future aspiration attainment (Polachek, 1975). Finally, they may perceive that if they significantly increased the level at which they fulfilled and performed ever-present (higher status) career demands, the time and energies needed to do so would generate serious conflict from their husbands (out of rivalry or perceived costs to them), thus making wives' own attainments extremely costly.

Whatever the causes and consequences of the contradiction, it is undoubtedly a very painful one. However, to the extent that the discrepancy is caused by reasons such as the three above, it is not necessarily a permanent feature of women's employment. It is possible to foresee that in the future such "causes" could become less pervasive, and thus the aspiration-expectation disparity could be reduced. Eventually the association between the two variables could become a positive one, as is presently the case with regard to the orientations they hold for husbands.

Work as a Right. Nonetheless, in spite of that current paradox, one may argue that achievement orientations, along with intertwined career definitions, are additional indicators of the degree to which work is defined as a right. Part of the basis for that argument lies with those factors that influence achievement and career orientations: sex-role preferences, tangible resources (education, job status, income), along with intangible resources, and so forth. Women who score high on these kinds of determinants may be said to assign greater significance and importance to their occupational activities. Work is not merely an option to be exercised at the whim of circumstances (family's material needs), or of husband's preferences ("it's not convenient for me to have you out of the house").

But quite apart from the elements that influence them, achievement and career orientations themselves inherently reflect the meaning of work. Movement along the continuum from option to right is stimulated by a high evaluation of one's own current work performance, by higher occupational aspirations and (expectations), and most emphatically by holding a career. Women who hold stronger achievement orientations take their work seriously enough to want to improve their performance levels to a significant degree. Holding a career means great investments of time and energy to obtain gratifications besides money.

It seems apparent that such women are too far enmeshed or caught up with some of the major ramifications of labor-force involvement to define it as mere option. Whether they originally intended it to turn out that way or not, they have now moved into the "rights" sector of the continuum of work meanings. For them work is becoming ever more significant and important—increasingly rewarding both at the tangible and intangible levels. Correspondingly, as well be developed more fully, it is becoming something that they will not easily relinquish. And by definition, that is a right.

Career Preferences and Job Satisfactions

Along with the finding that some women are already in occupations they believe are careers, is the reality that many women may find themselves excluded from the kinds of occupational opportunities they actually desire. Because of discrimination and gender-stereotypical socialization, some women may be working at jobs when they prefer careers. Others may be deeply dissatisfied with the benefit levels supplied by their occupations. They may feel relatively deprived compared to what men receive for comparable efforts or compared to what they could be getting had they been able to be more labor-force consistent over the years.

To explore these kinds of issues, respondents were probed on both their occupational preferences and satisfactions. For instance, after they stated whether their occupations were "careers" or "jobs," working wives were immediately queried, "Would you prefer it to be a career or job?" The percentage of workers responding in the "career" category increased from 42 to 58 percent; those responding in the "job" situation dropped from 58 to 42 percent. Clearly, while more workers currently have jobs than careers (58 to 42 percent), *more women would prefer to have careers than jobs* (58 to 42 percent). They are not dissuaded by the kinds of costs involved in unremunerated hours or in absence from domestic interactions. The desirability of career situations to these wives can be further demonstrated when it is observed that among all those who now hold careers, 92 percent prefer to continue in that situation. Only a handful preferred shifting to jobs. In contrast, among those who now have jobs, 31 percent would prefer shifting to careers.

The same kind of issue was probed among nonworkers. Words identical to those that described career-job differences to workers were read to nonworkers. They were then asked: "Which do you think you would prefer—a career or a job?" This item makes sense in view of the amount of occupational turnover that many women experience. Some current nonworkers held occupations at one or more points in the past. Some of them will eventually reenter the labor force. But whether or not they have any immediate plans to do so, they presumably carry with them some image or set of preferences about the sort of occupation they would like to choose should they ever (again) become workers. In this particular instance, would they prefer the less demanding routines of a job, or the more costly, yet rewarding satisfactions of a career? The distribution of responses is almost evenly split: 48 percent of nonworkers favor a career; 52 percent a job. One might have expected that more of these nonworkers would have leaned toward the more easily managed job situation, but surprisingly that was not the case.

Among both sets of wives, sex roles emerge as a strong influence on career preferences (table 2-3). However, external resources is an even more robust predictor. Workers who have more resources and who are more egalitarian are most likely to prefer a career occupation. Such women are more strongly oriented towards the gratifications of such occupations, feel they have the capabilities to manage them, and are more prepared for their inherent costs. The same sorts of theoretical ideas apply to nonworkers.

However, the relationships are not as strong as among workers, emphasizing once more the distinction between women actively involved in the labor force and those who are not. While there are similarities in certain kinds of patterns, significant differences remain as to the degree of their development. To the extent that career preferences represent the idea that working is a right, that notion is much more developed among workers than nonworkers.

Occupational Satisfactions. Similarly, to be more or less satisfied with one's occupation—hours, pay, chances to get ahead, and so forth—is relevant only to current workers and is explained in table 2-3.[16] Women who now actually hold a career and work primarily for enjoyment are more satisfied than wives who have jobs and work because they need the money. Not surprisingly, the literature shows that higher-status, career-oriented men are more occupationally satisfied than lower-status men (Kalleberg, 1977). Likewise, better-educated, sex-role-modern, career-oriented women have, over the years, been able to gain higher job statuses and incomes. As a result, they are more occupationally satisfied. Being more career-oriented has meant more benefits and thus made them more satisfied. But in feedback fashion, being more satisfied makes them more determined to maintain their careers.

Therefore, it is undoubtedly true that discrimination keeps some women out of the job market, catches some workers in jobs when they would prefer careers, and simultaneously reduces their work satisfactions. But it is also the case that some women are relatively less deprived than others. They work at careers or else will transfer into one as soon as possible, and they are relatively satisfied with the benefits their work supplies.

Work as a Right. Hence, for the rationales presented above, explaining why being in a career is an indication that work is defined as a right, so career preference may be taken as the same type of indicator. Similarly, relatively higher job satisfaction is another indicator that work is likely to be viewed more as a right than as an option. The rationale here is analogous to that used for intangible resources. Situations that are actually profitable are less likely to be viewed in merely optional or indifferent terms. Indifference is more likely where the situation is less profitable. Where it is profitable, Actor will be less willing to relinquish it, more eager to retain it, more concerned that it be viewed as something that is "inherently" hers or his. And over the years the more strongly women come to define work that way (as a right), the more likely they are to maintain (increase) extensive and intensive labor-force involvement. Thus, inseparably interwoven with intangible resources, achievement orientations, and career definitions as indicators of the meaning of work are career preferences and occupational satisfactions.

Occupational Priorities

Relative Importance

Just as sex-role preferences are the thread which binds those several elements into a coherent and systematic approach to the meaning of work, so they also incorporate the various dimensions of occupational priorities displayed in tables 2-4 and 2-5.

In the past, even when women worked, it was generally assumed that such activity had lower priority than husbands' work demands (Spiegel, 1957). Since the husband was often the sole, or at least ultimate, provider it was thought that in the event of a clash of job demands, it was in the best interests of the household to allow his to take precedence. Indeed, many women may simply have avoided employment because they were aware of the competing demands in time and energies that might ensue. It often seemed wiser not to generate those tensions.

Analogous to the greater significance of husbands' job demands as opposed to any job demands of wives, is the significance of children and their demands. It was generally held that children's demands take precedence over any interests that women themselves might hold—occupational interests in particular. Since the husband was ultimately responsible for the family's economic well-being, it did not appear in the family's best interests to allow children's demands to undercut his occupational activity and achievements. But since the wife did not share that ultimate responsibility, she was not similarly shielded from the demands of childcare. Indeed she was the chief caretaker of children.

From both perspectives—husbands' as well as children's interests—any paid employment of her own held lower priority. It was an option ringed with contingencies related to the well-being of others in the household. For working to have been her right, those priorities could not have differed that much in weight.

Therefore, to explore the issue of occupational priorities, wives were asked, "Would you say your job is *more* important to you personally than your husband's job, or is your own job *less* important to you personally than your husband's job, or are both jobs *equally* important to you?" (For simplicity's sake I shall use job and occupation interchangeably in the following pages unless a career orientation is specifically in view.) Here the working wife is asked to rank the relative importance to her of her own and her husband's occupation. Fifty-one percent said it was equally important; 33 percent said hers was less important; and 16 percent indicated it was actually more important. It is surprising and instructive that fully two-thirds of these workers consider their own occupations equally or more important to them than their husbands' occupations.

Table 2-4
Influences on Relative Occupational Importance, Husband Geographic Mobility, and Priority of Unintended Pregnancy, by Employment Status

Workers (n = 162)					
Wife's Occupation is Equal to or More Important than Husband's			*Husband Geographic Mobility*		
	beta	r		beta	r
1975 TW modernity	.27	.35	1975 PHA modernity	+.37	.36
Continuity	.15	.22	Husband income	−.27	−.18
Career	.16	.29	Husband education	+.13	.10
Catholic	.05*	.01	Catholic	−.01*	.02
$MR = .42, R^2 = .18$			$MR = .44, R^2 = .20$		

Workers (Fecund, n = 120)					
Pregnancy Hindrance – Family			*End Pregnancy or Cope*		
	beta	r		beta	r
Child-difference	.18	.23	Hindrance-family	.26	.31
Parity 75	.14	.27	1975 RLM modernity	.22	.21
1971 Economic satisfaction	−.17	−.24	Education	−.21	−.19
1971 PHA modernity	−.17	−.19			
Marriage-length	.16	.20			
Catholic	.15	.18			
$MR = .45, R^2 = .21$			$MR = .41, R^2 = .17$		
Pregnancy Hindrance-Woman			*End or Cope*		
	beta	r		beta	r
1975 TW modernity	.29	.30	1975 RLM modernity	.30	.28
Child-difference	.21	.24	Education	−.21	.16
Internal resource	−.19	−.19	Job satisfaction	−.10*	.19
			Catholic	−.07*	.12
			Hindrance-Woman	+.04*	.11
$MR = .41, R^2 = .17$			$MR = .38, R^2 = .15$		

Nonworkers (n = 233)		
Husband Geographic Mobility		
	beta	r
1975 TM modernity	+.22	.19
1971 Economic satisfaction	−.17	−.24
Husband income	−.12	−.17
Education	−.11	−.18
Catholic	+.02*	.03
$MR = .45, R^2 = .21$		

All betas significant at .05, unless starred.

Table 2-5
Influences on Priority of Unintended Pregnancy, for Fecund Nonworkers
(n = 167)

Pregnancy Hindrance-Family	beta	r		End Pregnancy or Cope	beta	r
1971 Economic				1970 Husband income	+.22	.26
satisfactions	−.17	−.27		1975 SA modernity	+.20	.23
1975 SA modernity	+.16	.19		1971 Birth intentions	−.15	−.18
1971 Birth intentions	−.20	−.21		1971 Age last child	−.15	−.19
1975 Unwanted children	+.18	.17		Current aspirations		
Husband education	−.10*	−.21		for husband	+.12	.17
$MR = .42, R^2 = .17$				$MR = .42, R^2 = .18$		

Pregnancy Hindrance-Woman	beta	r		End or Cope	beta	r
1975 SA modernity	+.25	.26		1975 SA modernity	+.21	.25
1971 Economic				1970 Husband income	+.22	.23
satisfaction	−.25	−.26		Catholic	−.12	−.08
Child-difference	+.19	.19		Hindrance-woman	+.12	.19
1971 Parity	+.17	.20				
External resources	+.15	.14				
$MR = 47, R^2 = .22$				$MR = .36, R^2 = .13$		

All betas significant at .05, unless starred.

The first section of table 2-4 shows those variables that predict a response in the direction of more or equal importance to wives. The strongest influence emerges from the 1975 traditional-wife (TW) sex role: the more egalitarian wives are on that role, the more likely they are to rank their own occupations as greater than or equal in importance to their husbands' jobs. Less TW modernity (more traditional sex-role preferences) predicts a tendency to rank wives' jobs as less important than husbands' jobs.

The traditional-wife role defines the degree to which interests of the wife are subordinate to those of husband and children. Women who reject that traditional role and thus express stronger preferences for equality of interests and for role interchangeability are more likely to report that their job is of equal or greater significance to them than their husbands' job. While in terms of sheer dollars most of their husbands may currently earn more than they do, there are important intrinsic gratifications at stake which these women consider crucial indeed. Thus, irrespective of any objective income differential, preferences for intangible individualistic gratifications and the relative significance of their occupations are strongly associated.

In addition, continuity and holding a career also predict greater or equal job importance. Wives who worked more months during the 1971-75 interval (see chapter 1), and who also define their occupations as careers, are more likely to place greater significance on their own occupations. Greater work frequency makes one's job loom that much more important. Continuing to receive extrinsic and intrinsic occupational rewards tends to increase the significance of those rewards. They become as crucial as benefits supplied by husbands. Similarly, to label one's occupation as "career" is by definition to rank certain gratifications as extremely worthwhile. Those gratifications, when juxtaposed with husbands' inputs, do not emerge second-best. Instead, because career elements are so meaningful and personally salient to these workers, they emerge as equally, and sometimes more, important to maintain.

Geographic Mobility

Another way to explore the issue of the significance of wives' versus husbands' occupations is through this item: "If you took a job that meant your family would have to move, would your husband be willing to move with you so that you could take that job?" This question taps a very practical yet highly critical matter and one that has been cited in the literature as a key element in determining the extent to which males are genuinely egalitarian (see Mortimer et al., 1976, for a review). Since, as the argument goes, in the past women have been amenable, often at considerable cost, to follow their husbands when they changed jobs, men who now claim to be egalitarian ought to be willing to bear similar costs that might be attached to their behaving reciprocally.

A substantial minority (32 percent) of all wives in the sample respond that their husbands would indeed follow them. Another 62 percent say they would not, while 6 percent are not sure. Table 2-4 explains husband compliance among workers. The strongest influence turns out to be the 1975 problematic-husband-alterations-dimension (PHA) (figure 1-1): the more these wives prefer individualistic gratifications (role interchangeability) in terms of this aspect of husband behavior, the more likely they are to believe that their husbands would actually follow them. (Sex-role modernity is also the strongest predictor of perceived husband willingness to follow nonworkers.)

Expecting shifts away from traditional husband prerogatives and privileges in general influences women to think that on this specific issue their husbands would indeed be willing for the costs involved. Very likely, workers who are more PHA-modern have had considerable experience in negotiating with their husbands regarding domestic responsibilities and the occupational demands of each spouse. Therefore, this fund of bargaining experience may be "causing" them to believe that they could successfully (from their standpoint) negotiate with their husbands over this vital matter as well.

It is particularly intriguing to note the opposite yet significant influences of husband-status variables. The more money their husbands earn, the more likely women are to respond negatively—their men would not move. But greater male education has precisely the opposing consequences—a positive response—they would move. These education and income variables are correlated at .36, so one might have expected them to influence willingness for mobility in the same fashion, but that is not the case. Income shows a more powerful effect than does education, suggesting that the more costly in terms of sheer dollars it is for men to follow their wives, the less likely they are to do so.

Leaving a financially rewarding situation for one that is more uncertain "merely" to fulfill wives' occupational aspirations is something relatively few men appear prepared to do. It simply is not a traditional male behavior pattern; to them it appears to be unprofitable—high costs, low rewards. Nevertheless, when men have more years of schooling, wives feel more confident that they could negotiate them into such a move. As indicated before, better-educated males are more egalitarian—more amenable to the individualistic aspirations of their wives. But the optimum situation for wives to achieve the goal of getting their husbands to follow them seems to be one where husbands' income is relatively lower and their education relatively higher. And being PHA-modern could be the catalyst leading them to try to negotiate such an issue in a fashion that is equitable to both partners.

Both the "relative importance of wife's job vs. husband's job," and the "husband geographic mobility" issues are useful indicators of the meaning of work. In the first instance, ranking an occupation as having priority at least equal in import to the husband's, means that it can be taken no less casually than his. His job is not an option—it is at least a right. Therefore, if hers is as important or significant as his, then it too must be taken just as seriously—it is her right.

Similarly, husband mobility to accommodate the wife's occupational endeavors has presumably been exceedingly rare. Its rarity underscores the pervasiveness of the option definition attached to women's work. When a woman reports it would occur, that would seem to be a particularly keen and sensitive indicator that she is not merely indifferent to her work. It is not (or is no longer) an option; it is indeed her right. When women are willing to experience what are virtually certain to be tough negotiations with their husbands in hopes of achieving their ends, their work must mean a very great deal to them. (Compare chapters 4 and 5.)

In both instances, (mobility, relative import) sex-role preferences continue to play the significant part that they did earlier. The more egalitarian women are, the higher they consistently rank (on indicators of work meaning) in the direction of defining work as their right.

Unintended Pregnancy as Priority

Besides the greater priority that husbands' occupational interests traditionally held over wives' interests, children's interests also held greater significance than those of the wife-mother. To try to assess the extent to which that pattern persists, a series of four items was developed and read sequentially only to women who reported they were fecund at the time of the 1975 interview.[17]

The first item was: "Some women get pregnant sooner than they would like to or at the wrong time. If that happened to you in the next five years, how much do you think that would hinder your plans to improve your family's living standard? Would that hinder your plans very much, some, or not much at all?" (The percentages were 14, 31, 55, respectively; $n = 312$). Item 2: "Would you be more likely to end the pregnancy or give up some of the things you wanted for your family?" Seven percent said they would "end" it, 75 percent responded "give up." Another 18 percent volunteered comments which were coded under a category labeled "cope somehow."

The third item shifts from family to individual concerns. "How much would such a pregnancy hinder your own work plans, plans for school, or anything else that concerns you personally as distinct from your family? Would you say that would hinder your plans very much (18 percent), some (33 percent), or not much at all (49 percent)?" Finally, item 4: "Would you be more likely to end the pregnancy (8 percent) or give up your own plans (79 percent)?" Another 13 percent responded they would "cope somehow."

Items 1 and 2 are designed mainly to sensitize the respondent to the distinction between household interests and the individualistic interests represented by items 3 and 4. In the first two items the woman must decide whether an unintended pregnancy would adversely influence the family's economic well-being, and therefore what her response to that pregnancy would be. But in the last two items the issue becomes the potentially negative consequences of such a pregnancy on her own occupational and/or educational interests, and therefore how she would respond to that pregnancy situation. It was expected that women who held modern sex-role preferences would be more likely to see such a pregnancy as inimical to their own interests and thus would be more likely to end it, or else cope, but not give up their plans. Note that the phrase "end the pregnancy" is a euphemism to describe induced abortion.

Item 1. Table 2-4 displays the determinants of item 1 among workers. Not surprisingly, the strongest influence is a measure of the difference between unintended pregnancies in 1971 and 1975.[18] The greater the difference (or the more unintended children during the interval), the greater the perceived hindrance. Greater 1975 parity (number of children) has the same effect. In short, wives who have already experienced the most unwanted pregnancies, and who also currently have more children, are most likely to see yet another unintended child as being very harmful to their family's financial situation. That situation is already strained, as suggested by the economic satisfactions variable[19] that appears in the equation: the less economically satisfied they were in 1971, the more hindrance they see an additional unplanned child to be in 1975.

PHA modernity (compare figure 1-1) predicts less potential hindrance.

Analogous to husband geographic mobility, PHA-modern women might expect to gain greater concessions from their husbands in the event of such a pregnancy. For example, they may expect to be able to negotiate their husbands into accepting childcare arrangements that would enable wives to continue working, and thus keep on contributing to the family's living standard.

Item 2. Table 2-4 displays determinants of Item 2. (Religious-legitimization-of-the-mother role (RLM) modernity (figure 1-1) appears to maintain strong influence in one direction while, unexpectedly, education moves in the opposite direction. Women who are more sex-role egalitarian are more likely to respond that they would "end" the pregnancy, or else "somehow cope." Since modernity on RLM implies a secular view of marriage institutions and of motherhood, it follows that such views would make abortion that much more acceptable. Given a clash of interests between family economic well-being and the costs of having an unintended child, persons who are RLM-modern appear more likely to choose abortion or else devise some means or strategies to cope with the unplanned pregnancy/birth so as, in either case, not to have to give up their plans.

But education influences women to give up the intended lifestyle plans. Such persons are more likely to be better off economically and are also likely to have fewer children. Therefore, prospects for an unplanned child and of having to sacrifice certain lifestyle elements do not emerge as overly costly. Given that education and RLM modernity are positively correlated (.21), it would appear that these two forces pull women in opposite directions.

The data further suggest that any such struggle is resolved by the degree to which the unintended pregnancy was perceived as a hindrance: the more inimical it is, the more wives are likely to end the pregnancy or cope with it in some way so as not to have to give up their plans. But the table shows that two strong predictors of perceived hindrance are family size and past unplanned children. Women who already have high child costs are least likely to want to incur still more child costs as a result of giving up certain lifestyle aspirations.

Item 3. After responding to items 1 and 2, item 3 draws for the respondent, hopefully, a sharp contrast between family lifestyle interests and her own individualistic interests. The related section of table 2-4 verifies the theoretical expectation that role-modern women would consider an unintended pregnancy as "very much" of a hindrance to their own interests. The more strongly they hold to individualistic interests or preferences for role interchangeability (as indicated by being less traditional on the traditional-wife gender role in 1975), the more likely they are to respond that the costs of an unintended pregnancy would be severe indeed. Moreover, as previously noted, the greater the number of unintended children they have had recently, the more likely they are to indicate that yet another would be exceedingly costly.

However, the internal resource variable has the opposite effect. Women who possess greater resources of the sort that enable them to negotiate and bargain effectively with their husbands are more likely to respond that the child would not be a hindrance. Evidently, these kinds of resources stimulate them to believe that they would somehow be able to cope with that eventuality. Perhaps, for instance, they could negotiate their husbands into sharing childcare responsibilities (including who is responsible for getting outside care), and thus they would not have to give up their current occupations. In that sense, the effect of internal resources is analogous to the prior impact of PHA modernity.

It is intriguing to observe that sex-role modernity has different consequences for collective well-being (item 1) than for individualistic well-being (item 3). In the former instance, modern PHA preferences (figure 1-1) suggest efforts by wives to involve husbands in domestic responsibilities, and thus to ameliorate the costs of unplanned pregnancies. By way of contrast, when their own interests are much more highlighted, the effect of gender modernity (traditional-wife) is to pinpoint or exacerbate the potential costliness of such a pregnancy. Indeed PHA itself correlates positively (+.23) to item 3 whereas it correlates negatively to item 1. As is the case for TW, to be more egalitarian on PHA is to perceive greater hindrance.

Item 4. Once those individualistic costs are underscored, the data suggest that role-modern women are less likely to subordinate their own interests to those of an unplanned child. The more modern (or individualistic) they are on RLM during 1975 (figure 1-1) the more likely they are to respond in the direction of either ending or coping with the pregnancy. Conversely, more traditional wives are more likely simply to give up their plans.

Whether years ago any working wives would have placed individualistic interests ahead of or on the same plane with child interests in the fashion indicated here is not certain. Very likely there were not many who did, while the proportion of those who do has presumably increased and will likely to continue to increase. This is because gender modernity predicts such behavior and evidence cited in chapter 1 indicates trends towards greater modernity. In short, as women workers come to prefer individualistic interests more strongly, occupational pursuits become defined more powerfully as a right. As an indicator of that type of definition, their own work takes on greater significance or priority vis-à-vis children. This would seem to hold both for reductions in the overall number that such women intend to have (Scanzoni, 1975b), as well as in willingness to terminate pregnancies that are perceived as hindrances to their goal attainment.

Or if they do not terminate, they will somehow devise strategies to cope with such situations, perhaps in what some have called "Supermom" fashion or else by pressing for greater childcare concessions from their husbands. Since gender modernity has sensitized them to the costs of these situations, what is increasingly less likely to occur is the traditional reaction of merely giving up either their family lifestyle aspirations or their own individualistic interests.

Nonworkers. Interestingly, there are no significant differences between fecund workers and nonworkers on items 1 through 4. That is, nonworkers appear just as likely as workers to perceive hindrances to collective and individualistic interests and just as likely to react in similar ways. Even more important are the basic similarities between the patterns displayed in tables 2-4 and 2-5. The self-actualization (SA) gender-role dimension (figure 1-1) appears repeatedly in table 2-5, generating theoretically expected outcomes. First, egalitarian non-workers are more likely to define unplanned pregnancies as hindrances both to household and especially individual interests. Second, such women are also more likely to refuse to subordinate their interests to those of that particular unintended event.

In other words, nonworkers are remarkably like workers insofar as the issues of occupational significance versus child significance are concerned. The crucial question is: does sex-role modernity indicate greater willingness to rank occupational or other personal interests at least at par with those of an additional child? Even though they are not now employed, the response is affirmative. The consistent appearance in table 2-5 of the innovative SA dimension implies a linkage between possible future occupational plans and willingness to remove or else effectively cope with potential threats to those plans. Like workers, their individualistic aspirations militate against merely giving up those plans and the gratifications inherent in them.

Work As a Right. Women who perceive unintended children as a hindrance to their own individualistic interests, and who refuse to relinquish or subordinate their interests to that contingency, may be said to define work more as a right than an option. That pattern of not subordinating their own interests to those of a child contingency indicates they are not indifferent to work—it is not a mere option to be laid down and picked up in accordance with child constraints. Conversely, to subordinate their own interests is clearly the traditional "thing to do." That subordination indicates the relative casualness or indifference with which many women presumably tended to approach work. That lesser priority also indicates work's traditional unimportance as compared to the highly significant maternal duty to bear and care for children. Refusing to acknowledge the widely accepted greater priority of maternal over occupational behaviors suggests a desire on the part of at least some women to define work as their inherent right.

Moreover, as was the case with regard to wife interests versus husband interests, sex-role preferences are a pivotal stimulant that move women to accord at least as much priority to their own interests as they do the interests of children. Women who are more egalitarian appear more likely to try to maintain equivalency of well-being—to balance collective and individualistic concerns (Ekeh, 1974).

Summary and Conclusions

Ever since white married women have been entering the paid labor force, their work has been defined as an option. It was an activity they did contingent on the premise that it would not harm family interests in general and, more specifically, the well-being of husband and children.

The meaning of work is a continuum with several points shading into one another. At one extreme is the idea of prohibition—a married woman should not work at all. Though that idea was once prevalent, its acceptance today is presumably quite minimal, and was not considered in the chapter. To its left is option, followed by work as a right. A right is legitimate behavior—behavior which can be contravened by others only with the greatest of effort, often conflict. It is "what no one can take from you." The central arguments of this chapter are that some married women do define work as a right, that this definition is stimulated by sex-role preferences and, given shifts towards modernity in those preferences, that increasing numbers of women are coming to define work as a right.

Several dimensions were set forth as indicators of this gradual evolution in meaning. All of them share at least two common threads: they are related to the idea that work is rewarding, and they are stimulated directly or indirectly by modern sex-role preferences. These dimensions include intangible resources, occupational achievement orientations, career definitions and preferences, occupational satisfactions, husband's geographic mobility on wife's behalf, priority of wife's occupation versus husband's occupation, and priority of wife's interests versus potentially negative and disruptive consequences of an unintended pregnancy.

These features indicate where work is located on the meaning-of-work continuum. Women who rank high or strongly on these factors may be said to define work more as right than as option. Lower or weaker rankings indicate that work means option more than right.

It is quite possible that over the course of their lives, these women have experienced an evolution or development in their own views of work. Given the data in chapter 1 that they became significantly more egalitarian by 1975 than they had been in 1971, it is quite likely that they also changed with respect to the several dimensions of work-meaning explored here. Presumably over each dimension they shifted in the direction of defining work more as right than as option. The evolution of these meanings is in part traceable to the prior "flow" their lives. Their 1971 sex-role preferences helped stimulate extensive and sive work involvement which later increased their egalitarianism (Scanzoni,). And while that sort of feedback was occurring, the meaning that they attached to work was probably also being affected. The more payoffs (tangible and intangible) that work was providing, the more it became something that they felt ought not to be subject to the whim of extraneous contingencies. Instead it became something that was legitimately their own. It was something that they felt they ought to pursue in spite of, and in the face of, pressures such as sexist discrimination and resistance from husband and/or children.

In effect, work was becoming a right. That evolution occurred because of prior events including work activity and gender egalitarianism. But at the same time, it can be safely assumed that defining work that way virtually is bound to increase both work involvement and egalitarianism.

In that same vein, evidence from chapter 1 suggests that there is an overall shift in American society, especially on the part of younger well-educated women, to adopt more individualistic sex-role preferences. Given that likelihood, it can be said that women's defining their own work as a right is more pervasive as well as more strongly held in contemporary America than was true ten or twenty years ago. And since we have every reason to expect that egalitarian sex-role preferences will continue to become more widespread in the future, we can also expect women to continue to rank increasingly closer toward the work-as-right position on these seven (and other related) dimensions. That is, we can expect continual ongoing changes in the form of larger numbers of women holding greater amounts of intangible resources, higher achievement orientations, stronger career definitions and preferences, higher occupational satisfactions, and gaining more frequent husband mobility on wives' behalf, as well as holding stronger priorities for wives' occupations as compared to husbands' occupations and children's interests.

The theoretical perspective used to help guide the chapter's arguments is an eclectic form of utilitarian, reward-cost, or purposive-action theory. Its basic premise is that persons are profit-seeking; that is, they seek to maximize benefits and avoid costs. Sex-role preferences are one way to identify variation in women's goals or interests. Women who prefer a high degree of gender-role egalitarianism prefer one set of rewards; women who are more traditional prefer another set. Given that variation it was predicted that the preferences of modern women would lead them to fall toward the work-as-right position on each of the dimensions used to assess the meaning of work. Similarly, the preferences of traditional women would influence them to remain where traditional women have always been—at the option end.

I began this chapter by saying that an increase in the proportions of employed women was in itself not an indicator of significant marital change. What is much more crucial is the underlying meaning that women attach to their own paid employment. If it remains at the level of option, few changes in family structure will have occurred even though more women may exercise the option. However, if more women are defining it ever more strongly as a right, then indeed significant changes would be taking place in contemporary marriage.

The thrust of this chapter is that such changes are indeed occurring in gradual evolutionary fashion. Not only is shift in meaning from option to right a significant change in and of itself, it is also extremely significant because of what it portends for fundamental changes in marital structure. Definition of women's employment as a right contributes towards the decreasing predominance of the sharp role differentiation that for many decades has been the prime structural feature of marriage. The more widely and strongly women's employment is defined as a right, the more it may be said that marriages are moving away from being characterized by differentiation and, instead, are becoming characterized by actual role interchangeability. That specific theme will be pursued in the next chapter as I take up the *consequences* of women's employment.

Notes

    1. Factor-loadings for each dimension are keyed to figure 2-1. *External:* B .44, E .52, F .40, G .62, I .70, N .44, O .46, P .49, Q .58, R .53. *Internal:* H .57, K .54, T .47, U .52. *Appreciation:* L .68, M .67. ALPHAS (reliability coefficients): External = .83, Internal = .67, Appreciation = .81.

    2. r's: mother's education = .33; father's education = .34; father's job status = .27. (Measure of job status is Duncan Socioeconomic Index (SEI).

    3. $r = .27$.

    4. Traditional-wife 1975 r = .39; SA 1975 = .29; PHA 1975 = .31; TH 1975 = .25; RLM 1975 = .25; TM 1975 = .25.

    5. r's: education = .25, TW 1975 = .29; RLM 1975 = .21.

    6. r's of daughter's education with mother's education = .39; with father's education = .29 (workers). Nonworkers, κ's, respectively, = .31, .29.

    7. r's: workers = .46; nonworkers = .48.

    8. r's: workers = .61; nonworkers = .34.

    9. The logic followed to arrive at what variables should be used as explanatory variables in chapters 2, 3, 4, and 5 is simple and straightforward. In this particular instance, the question is which variables out of the very many available to us show significant correlations with occupational evaluations? In research such as this which is essentially exploratory, it is premature to try to fit a prior model to the data. Too much is as yet unknown regarding the issues in question to permit that constraining strategy. Therefore, variables showing significant correlations with the variable to be explained are placed in a series of stepwise regression equations to discover the ones that have the strongest beta weights and account for the most explained variance in that dependent variable. Finally, the independent variables that consistently demonstrate the greatest predictive power are placed into the "regular" regression equations displayed in tables throughout the various chapters. The ways in which those independent and dependent variables were measured are explained in notes the first time the particular variable is discussed in the text.

10. For example, among women who worked at both the 1971 and 1975 interviews, their 1971 SA score showed a beta of .30 in explaining 1975 income. The only predictor in the equation that was stronger was 1970 income, beta = .46.

11. "Is the *main* reason you work now because your family needs the money or because you enjoy working?" The r of "working for enjoyment" and 1975 TW modernity is .24.

12. As indicated by table 1-3, there is a high degree of correlation among most of the sex-role dimensions, especially in 1975. Thus, any one of them may be taken as an indicator of the larger construct described in chapter 1 as "degree of preferred gender-role differentiation." And just as note 9 argued that it is premature to model relationships among certain or specific independent and dependent variables, it is equally premature to try to predict which of the several sex-role variables as measured either in 1971 or 1975 will affect particular dependent variables but not others. Therefore, in each instance throughout these several chapters, I will examine the correlations between all of the sex-role dimensions and the particular dependent variable, and select the one with the strongest significant association to use in the regression equations. Whichever one is used, that particular sex-role variable is an indicator of the larger relationship between preferred gender-role differentiation and Y. Wherever it is relevant, I shall try in my discussion to identify any particular significance to having TW as opposed to SA or perhaps TH predict a certain dependent variable.

13. Measure of job status throughout the book is in terms of the Duncan SEI.

14. Among women who worked at both interview points, their education was the strongest predictor, followed by TW 1971 without 1971 SEI in the equation. Since education and TW are related (r = .25), it appears that modern sex role preferences operate on subsequent job status via education as well as directly.

15. Mean scores in table 2-2, $p < .05$.

16. "All things considered—such as hours, pay, chances to get ahead, and so forth—how satisfied are you with your present job? Would you say: very dissatisfied, dissatisfied, satisfied, or very satisfied?"

17. Measured by a series of items devised by Ryder and Westoff, 1971, and defined as the physiological capacity to reproduce.

18. Unintended pregnancies are measured by items devised by Ryder and Westoff, 1971.

19. "Economic satisfactions" is based on the following two-item index: (a) "How do you feel about the standard of living—the kind of income, clothing, car, opportunities for children, and so on—that your husband's job allows you to have? Do you feel very satisfied, satisfied, or dissatisfied?" (2) "Realistically speaking, how good do you think your chances are for getting ahead in life? Do you feel they are excellent, fair, or somewhat limited?"

3

Women and the Consequences of Work

Introduction

This chapter shifts our focus from work meanings to work *consequences*. In the past, women's employment had limited consequences for the institutions of marriage and family because, among other things, work had a limited meaning; it was viewed as nothing more than an option. Therefore, its consequences were generally restricted to helping carry the family through some financial pressures. Census figures for many years have shown that the lower the husband's income, the more likely the wife was to work. Thus, the "option" was apparently exercised more often in less affluent homes since the wife's working had greater consequences in alleviating those families' more frequent financial stringencies. But outside of that amelioration of financial stress, the consequences of women's employment for families in years past are not easily identified.

That uncertainty is particularly keen when women have shifted into the labor force in response to financial pressures and out again in response to the periodic easing of those pressures (F.D. Blau, 1975). However, when women exhibit greater continuity (relatively uninterrupted labor-force involvement), a possible consequence is enhancement of the family's basic living standard. That possibility is explored in this chapter, along with two other important potential consequences of wife employment: impact on the family's social class position; and impact on shared performance of household duties, including the duty to be coprovider.

The findings reported here indicate that women's work does indeed have consequences for all three areas. Furthermore, the variation in these consequences seems to be related, among other things, to degree of sex-role modernity. Years ago, there may have been less variation in the impacts of wives' employment because presumably there was less variation among women's sex-role preferences. Today, as women move in a more egaliatarian direction, changes in preferred costs and rewards, together with the definition of work as a right rather than an option, may be expected to have important repercussions for a family's living standard, for the social-class position it attains, and for the way it divides up household duties. In other words, the wife's employment may now have consequences corresponding to those that have been traditionally associated with the husband's employment (compare Oppenheimer, 1977).

The long-standing consequences of making it the male's obligation to work and provide for his family are many and varied. The family's lifestyle or living standard, for example, was largely dependent on his own income. This can be seen, for instance, in the traditional banking practice of extending a mortgage loan based on the husband's income, whether the wife works or not.

Second, the family's social class position has generally been based on the husband's job position. Whether the wife worked or not, all members of the household shared the same social level according to his inputs.

Third, the husband has been exempted from most domestic tasks such as cleaning, etc. Since the well-being of the household rested ultimately with him, he could not legitimately be required to perform domestic tasks as well. This was especially true if such performance might hinder his occupational endeavors.

If changes are taking place in all three of these areas as consequences of wives' working, we need to trace how such consequences might come about. Let us consider each area in turn.

Family Lifestyle

Besides being asked how satisfied they were with the living standard that their husband's job supplied, employed wives in the sample were asked, "Do you feel *your working* allows your family to have a higher standard of living than it could have if you did not work?"[1] Table 3-1 shows that the incomes of wives and husbands predict precisely opposite results. The higher the woman's own income, the more likely she is to respond "yes," her working does indeed promote a higher family lifestyle. But the larger her husband's income, the greater the tendency to reply in the negative.[2]

Two related factors shed some additional light on the matter. Wives who are more dissatisfied with their husband's lifestyle provision,[3] and who work mainly for money,[4] are more likely to indicate that their working enhances family lifestyle. Greater satisfaction with husband provision and being motivated to work for enjoyment show the opposite influence.

Thus, four factors point convincingly in a single direction. Wives' perceived contribution to family lifestyle depends on the dollars they supply relative to husbands' dollars, along with certain evaluations of their own occupation and their husband's occupation. The wives' 1971 sex-role preferences enter the picture in terms of their positive impact on wives' 1974 income, as explained in chapter 2.[5] In addition, we learn that women who prefer a career rather than a job also believe that their working influences family lifestyle. And recall from table 2-3 that women who were more sex-role modern were more likely to prefer careers.

Therefore, over the years preferences for sex-role egalitarianism contribute towards moving wives into the labor force, keeping them there (continuity) and positively influencing the obtaining of higher incomes. Subsequently, by 1975, the greater their own income is, the more they see themselves significantly enhancing family lifestyle.

Table 3-1

Influences on Women's Impact on Family Living Standard, by Employment Status

Workers						
Positive Consequences of Employment on Current Living Standard						
Employed 1975 (n = 162)			*Employed 1971 and 1975 (n = 112)*			
	beta	r			beta	r
Wife income	+.25	.31	Wives' income increase		.22	.34
1975 Economic satisfaction	−.15	−.27	Work for money		.31	.33
Work for money	+.22	.26	Prefer career		.19	.16
Prefer career	+.18	.18	1974 Husband's income		−.18	−.31
1974 Husband's income	−.16	−.23	1975 SA modernity		.15	.20
1975 SA modernity	+.10*	.16				

$MR = .51, R^2 = .26$ $MR = .53, R^2 = .28$

Positive Consequences of Employment on Future Living Standard (n = 162)

	beta	r
Current positive consequences	.40	.44
External resources	.13	.26
Current aspirations	.12*	.22
1975 SA modernity	.10*	.24

$MR = .51, R^2 = .26$

Nonworkers (n = 233)

Positive Consequences on Living Standard if Job Were Held

	beta	r
Negative peer evaluation	+.15	.20
Some 1974 income	+.14	.18
Worked 1971	+.12	.15
1974 Husband income	−.09*	−.18
Catholic	−.08*	−.09

$MR = .30, R^2 = .10$

All betas significant at .05, unless starred.

Nonetheless, the higher the husbands' income, the more difficult it is to define oneself as significantly enhancing family lifestyle or to be dissatisfied with husbands' economic inputs. Part of the reason for that conclusion is that husbands continue to earn substantially greater dollar amounts than wives. Therefore, significant contributions by wives to family lifestyles would seem to be in direct proportion to their capabilities to produce as much income as their husbands.

There is a considerable literature exploring job status and incomes of men

(Sewell and Hauser, 1975). No comparably vast literature exists for women, though some efforts are being made in that direction (Featherman and Hauser, 1976; McClendon, 1976; Trieman and Terrell, 1975; Scanzoni, 1979a). Until recently researchers were seldom interested in female job and income patterns since that did not appear to be a relevant theoretical or policy question. But to the degree women become "serious workers" in the sense that work becomes increasingly defined as their right, then those kinds of questions become pertinent indeed.

Given discrimination in hiring, advancement, and wages which women very often experience, together with variation in their degree of gender-role modernity, increases in women's job statuses and income could be somewhat problematic. For example, among all women who worked both in 1971 and 1975, their earlier mean-job-status score (SEI) was 44.8, while in 1975 their score was 46.3. While the latter score is slightly higher than before, the difference is not significant.

However, when earnings are compared for women who had incomes in both 1970 and 1974, the increase is significant. In 1970 their mean income was at just $4,000; by 1974 it had risen to just over $5,500, or about a 38 percent increase over four years. However, the mean earnings of their own husbands also rose significantly from approximately $8,500 in 1971 to approximately $13,500 in 1975, a gain of some 59 percent. Thus, while these women have made considerable dollar gains over the interval, they started out and remained behind their husbands.

In 1973 the mean earnings of white American wives (husband-present, under age 35, living in the North and West) who worked 50 to 52 weeks was $6,024 (U.S. Bureau of Census, 1975:40). Undoubtedly, by 1975 that national figure had risen at least $500, which would then make it virtually identical to the $6,600 1975 figure for comparable women in this sample who worked full time in 1975 (and had also worked in 1971). Therefore, the earnings of full-time women workers in the sample match those of women with comparable work involvement nationally.

And, like such women nationally, their earnings constitute more than 40 percent of their mean family incomes—quite a substantial amount. (Specifically, the figure is 44 percent, while the national figure was 43 percent in 1973. See U.S. Census Bureau, 1975:40.) Furthermore, these figures are part of a long-term trend toward greater contributions by women to family income. For instance, in 1968 wife's earnings nationally accounted for only 27 percent of family income, but that figure was up from 20 percent in 1958 (U.S. Bureau of Census 1970:3). Interestingly enough, in spite of her 1968 contribution, the Census report judged that "the working wife still remains a marginal contributor to family income . . . "

Later in this chapter some of the implications of husband-wife income-ratios will be probed, but for now two contrasting points emerge. On the one hand, there remains an overall income deprivation (both absolute and rate of increase) that working wives experience when compared to their husbands. But on the other hand when attention is focused on that subset of women who exhibit considerable continuity or work consistency over time—and who currently work full time—it turns out that the dollar contribution of such women to their families is substantial when compared to that of their husbands. Furthermore, Census data indicate a trend in the direction of an increase in the relative contribution that wives make. These contrasting and somewhat paradoxical themes must be understood in order to obtain a full-orbed grasp of the kinds of changes that are occurring in American (and Western) families, as well as the kinds of constancies that persist.

That sort of contrast is indicative of the transitional period through which family structures are currently passing. At present, gender-modern women who, for instance, state that they work chiefly for "enjoyment" or intrinsic purposes, tend to be married to higher-status men who earn relatively higher incomes. Therefore, in spite of their achievement aspirations as well as performances (compare chapter 2), their incomes only rarely approximate those of their husbands.[6]

In the future, it can be expected that sex discrimination will gradually decline, that younger women will begin career styles earlier in their lives (compare chapter 2), and will display more continuity than is presently the case. The result should be incomes more at par with their husbands.

Admittedly, because of discrimination and other factors it is difficult to imagine a time when wives would earn incomes comparable to husbands, but the following Census data might be a harbinger of the future. During 1975 white "year-round full-time workers" (18 to 24-year-old wives with husbands present) earned a mean income of $6,730. That figure is 87 percent of the 1975 mean income ($7,736) earned by comparable men with wives present (U.S. Bureau of Census, 1977:183). In short, young women who work just as much as young men earn almost as much as they do. Therefore, given all of the ideas discussed in chapter 2 regarding ongoing changes in the several dimensions that make up the meaning of work, it is not at all inconceivable that a future cohort of younger wives with as much continuity as men would report incomes similar to those of husbands. And as they aged, it is possible that those women would retain their continuity and thus retain comparable incomes.

At that future stage of evolutionary family development, one could expect to find a positive correlation between working for the intangible reasons that have always motivated serious workers of either sex (not merely for reasons of money to meet immediate needs) and enhancement of family lifestyle. Meanwhile, during the interim, as income gaps often remain largest where role modernity is greatest (because better-educated men are more sex-role egalitarian), one may expect to continue to discover actual living-standard increments supplied by women to be greatest when husbands earn relatively less money.

The import of enlarged wife inputs on lifestyle is further substantiated by examining consistent workers—those women who worked both at the 1971 and 1975 interviews. The related section of table 3-1 shows that the greater the difference between their 1974 and 1970 earnings, the more likely they are to report that their working does indeed enhance family lifestyle. It also turns out that the more modern their sex role preferences were in 1971, the greater the increase in their incomes by 1974.[7] Therefore, over the years ahead, it would seem that gender-modern women will continue to work more consistently, earn higher incomes, and contribute significantly to improvements in family lifestyle.

Yet these are precisely the women who are not motivated to work solely for money any more than men are. Thus, in the future we can expect to discover that intrinsic work motivations will be linked positively to lifestyle enhancement, instead of negatively as is now the case. Simultaneously, gender-traditional women of the future, who continue to report that they work mainly for money, should show a negative association with enhanced lifestyle, instead of the positive one that presently appears. This reversal can be expected to occur mainly because of the substantially greater incomes that gender-modern women will presumably be earning—incomes that absolutely should be much greater than those of traditional women, and relatively quite comparable to those of their husbands.

Future Lifestyle

In the related section of table 3-1, the question becomes, do workers expect their family lifestyle to be higher in five years because they are working?[8] They are asked to project whether or not their future efforts will, over time, raise their family's living standard. The time element is important for several reasons, not least of which is that it implies long-term commitment of some women to the labor force. Those not on a "working track" or who exhibit little continuity are not likely to believe they will be enhancing lifestyles. In contrast, those who worked in 1971, who worked most frequently during the past four years, and who might work more frequently throughout the next five, are the ones likely to expect to increase their incomes, and thus presumably embellish family lifestyle more significantly.

Clearly the four variables (and the elements that influence them) are indicative of that kind of long-term work involvement. The most powerful of the forces is current perceived enhancement: the more they see their own employment making a difference in lifestyle now, the more likely they are to see it making a lifestyle difference five years from now. Simultaneously, wives who possess higher levels of external resources, hold higher occupational aspirations, and hold modern sex-role preferences also maintain the same expectations.

Lifestyle of Nonworkers

Among 1975 nonworkers the issue of any type of wife impact on lifestyle had to be approached somewhat differently. These women were asked, "If you had a job, would your family's standard of living be higher than it is right now?" Significantly, almost two-thirds (61 percent) replied that it would be, whereas 39 percent said it would not. Therefore, in spite of current nonemployment, it is quite apparent that a substantial majority of these wives do believe that their own efforts could indeed raise their family's living standard.

Moreover, those variables that account for perceived enhancement, (table 3-1), while not as robust as those for workers, do provide useful insights. In the first place, current nonworkers who nonetheless had had some 1974 earnings, and who had also worked in 1971, are likely to respond positively about the consequences of their labor-force activity. Thus, analogous to workers, those who have been most active in the labor force are the ones most likely to expect that additional activity would make a difference. A second analogy is that the more dollars earned by their husbands, the more likely they are to respond that working would not make a difference.

Third, however, is a variable that did not appear among workers—the influence of peers' evaluations. All respondents were asked how their friends and relatives evaluated the standard of living that "your husband's job allows you to have." The data reveal that the more negatively significant others evaluate husbands' provision, the more likely nonworkers are to believe that they themselves could enhance family lifestyle.

Indeed, it may be that those negative evaluations will eventually become a cause of their seeking a job. It could therefore be predicted that a certain number of these wives will eventually enter or reenter the labor force in order to overcome those evaluations. In brief, peer influences could trigger a chain of influences resulting in improved family lifestyle, with possible implications for the social-class position of the household, an issue considered next.

Recap

In terms of this first consequence of women's work, it is clear that their working does have an impact on family lifestyle, as far as workers themselves are concerned. Whether or not their husbands would concur is open to investigation. But when, as was done here, wives' objective dollar contribution to family income is taken into account, it is difficult to assert that no lifestyle impact is taking place.

As might be expected, the lifestyle impact occurs most strongly when workers earn more dollars. And it is gender-modern wives who both earn more and also have more substantially increased their incomes over the past several years. Such women do not work primarily for money to meet immediate family expenses. Instead, they have a history of long-term work involvement with career overtones, including defining work as their right. Their employment carries with it the sorts of intrinsic elements examined in chapter 2. What complicates their impact on family lifestyle is that they tend to be married to egalitarian men who also earn more money. Therefore, the greater the disparity between the two objective dollar contributions, the less they perceive that lifestyle is substantially affected.

Nevertheless, throughout the remainder of their married lives, gender-modern, career-oriented women can be expected to continue to increase their earnings considerably. Therefore, their impact on lifestyle should increase correspondingly—especially if their husbands have already reached or will soon reach their earnings plateau. Finally, even most nonworkers believe that if they worked they would significantly affect their family's living standard.

The implications of these patterns for long-term family changes could be extraordinary. It seems safe to assume that increasing numbers of younger women will begin marriage with as much concern as men for occupational achievement (described in chapter 2). These wives probably will spend approximately as much time in the labor force as their husbands. After ten years, there should not be the income disparities now observed in most marriages due to women's lower continuity. Therefore, family lifestyle and potential consumption patterns would presumably be far more affluent than is generally the case today when usually only the husband is the main achiever.

Such families are likely to have fewer children, which would further increase consumption options (Scanzoni, 1975b). Should inflation continue to be the pervasive force that some economists predict for the foreseeable future, that factor (along with egalitarianism) would certainly be an additional impetus to this sort of dual-career lifestyle (Fogarty, et al., 1971). Therefore, over the long run, assessment of social-class position based solely on husbands' inputs would tend to become quite meaningless. But the question is, how meaningful are such assessments right now?

Social-Class Position of the Household

There has already been some attempt to incorporate wives' efforts into the assessment of household social position (Haug, 1973; Rossi, et al., 1974; Ritter and Hargens, 1975; Hiller and Philliber, 1978; Sampson and Rossi, 1975). The general consensus of that literature is that given the kinds of ongoing changes occurring in wives' preferences and behaviors, it makes much more sense to try to come up with indicators of social class based on both spouses' efforts, than to continue to rely on husbands' achievements alone. Therefore, what follows is an attempt to do exactly that—develop indicators of household position that take both workers' inputs into account.

The variable explained in the first section of table 3-2 is one that has been used for many years in numerous studies and is still being used (Laumann and Senter, 1976); the self-assignment by respondents to one of a list of "social class" categories.[9] There always has been and continues to be controversy surrounding the validity of this type of item. Nonetheless, to the extent that Americans carry some image of a series of differentiated social classes, an item such as this has proven to be a reasonably valid indicator of that differentiation. In that regard a recent empirical analysis (Kluegel, et al., 1977) shows that this type of item contains considerably more reliability and validity than had been formerly attributed to it.

Thus the issue becomes, why do respondents place themselves in the "lower," "working," "lower-middle," "upper-middle," or "upper" class? Women were asked to make this class assignment based on their husband's job alone. The table displays four variables that significantly influence the assessments of working wives. Their husbands' income is by far the most powerful: the more dollars males earn, the higher the class placement. Their husbands' job status also has a positive effect. In addition, the more satisfied they were with the living standard supplied by husbands, the higher the class placement.

This syndrome is clearly the traditional pattern said to determine social differentiation in the United States, and probably in most other industrialized nations as well (Laumann and Senter, 1976). Note, however, that external resources possessed by the wife also had a significant positive impact on class placement. Thus it can be argued that even when the investigator tries to restrict class assessment solely to husbands' efforts, variables unique to wives intrude to influence household position. This same generalization can be inferred from the section on nonworkers. Besides those predictors attached to husbands' efforts there is also the career-orientation variable. Nonworkers who prefer a career over a job (table 2-3) are more likely to place themselves in a higher social position.

To try to explain the impact of these unique wife variables, consider workers. Their external resources may be salient in at least three ways. First, some of the skills and capabilities useful in settings external to the household may also be applied to consumption behavior. Whether these women are primarily responsible for purchasing food and other items or share the duties with their husbands, some of them may possess greater skills than others in stretching their husbands' finite dollars to cover virtually infinite demands. The more such skills are possessed, the higher the lifestyle that the family can attain, and thus presumably the greater the social class placement. For instance, among wives of factory workers with comparable incomes, it is likely that some place themselves in the working class, others in the lower-middle class. In the latter cases, those wives may expend their money in such a way as to attain what they consider to be a middle-class lifestyle.

Table 3-2
Influences on Various Bases of Household Differentiation, by Employment Status

Social Class Based on Husband Efforts					
Workers (n = 162)			Nonworkers (n = 233)		
	beta	r		beta	r
Husband income	.33	.48	Husband income	.24	.49
Husband job status	.20	.39	Husband job status	.24	.47
External resources	.14	.28	Evaluation of		
1975 Economic			husband	.15	.40
satisfaction	.15	.36	Marriage-age	.16	.34
			1975 Economic		
			satisfaction	.16	.36
			Prefer career	.13	.26
$MR = .57, R^2 = .33$			$MR = .66, R^2 = .43$		

Workers (n = 162)					
Positive Impact of Wife Working on Class			Social Class Based on Efforts of Wife and Husband		
	beta	r		beta	r
Wife income	.26	.34	Family income	.21	.41
Husband class			External resources	.25	.40
placement	−.34	−.32	1975 Parity	−.15	−.24
Future Living			1975 Economic		
standard impact	.19	.28	satisfaction ·	.12	.26
Future			1971 Economic		
aspirations	.18	.25	satisfaction	.13	.30
			1971 SA modernity	.10	.26
$MR = .54, R^2 = .30$			$MR = .56, R^2 = .32$		

Nonworkers (n = 233)					
Positive Impact on Class if Job Were Held			Class Based on Efforts of Husband and Wife if Job Were Held		
	beta	r		beta	r
Wife's perceived impact			Husband income	.22	.38
on lifestyle	.27	.33	Husband education	.16	.35
Negative peer evaluation	.22	.33	Marriage-age	.17	.32
Evaluation of husband's			Future aspirations		
occupational performance	−.15	−.24	for husband	.15	.28
1975 SA modernity	.10	.13	Prefer career	.13	.24
			1971 TM modernity	.12	.20
$MR = .46, R^2 = .20$			$MR = .54, R^2 = .29$		

All betas significant at .05.

Second, external resources may be brought to bear in assisting husband job efforts by entertaining his work peers (figure 2-1, item b), or by assisting in other kinds of husband occupational activities that could possibly involve the wife. In these ways, wives who possess greater resources may be a positive asset to their husbands' occupations (especially those defined as careers), and thus obviously enhance household social position.

Finally, wives' external resources very likely overlap onto husbands' occupational efforts in the sense that they function as "colleagues"—especially since these are working women. Although P.M. Blau and Duncan (1967:359) could identify no factors by which wives affect husbands' occupational performance, resources of this type could turn out to have that consequence. Working women who are more effective in functioning outside the family may be better able to stimulate their husbands to do the same, thus ultimately contributing to social class position.

The impact of a preferred career orientation among nonworkers may be analogous to the earlier item (table 3-1) in which nonworkers felt they could enhance family lifestyle *if* they worked. In this case, it may be that some career-oriented wives are planning soon to go/return to work, and the expectation of that behavior may have a positive impact on household social position because of the inputs they expect to make.

In any case, it is evident that even when an attempt is made to measure social class in the traditional fashion, wives' resources, behaviors, and aspirations enter in. It thus appears virtually impossible to restrict perceived household class position solely to husbands' attainments. Women's efforts (particularly if they work) seem inevitably to enter in and make at least some positive contribution.

Wife's Impact on Social Position

Working wives were read the following item: "You said your husband's job places you in the ____ social class. Do you feel your working helps your family belong to a different social class?"[10] It turns out that the more dollars they earn, the more likely they are to respond positively—their working does indeed place them in a different (higher) class (table 3-2).[11]

Similarly, wives who believe their working will permit a higher family lifestyle in the future (compare table 3-1) also believe their working currently increases their family's social position. Simultaneously, a second future-oriented variable also helps explain why they think their working results in higher class position. That variable is higher occupational aspirations for the future (compare table 2-3). Nonetheless, the higher the social position wives are in already by virtue of their husbands' efforts, the less likely they are to indicate that their working would enhance that position.

This last connection is theoretically analogous to the prior discussion of why wives who state they work primarily for enjoyment are less likely to see family lifestyle increased. Better-educated, gender-modern women earn more money, which has the effect of enabling them to maintain "better" lifestyles or household consumption patterns. Enhancement of these patterns is a basis for their conclusion that they are able to improve on their husbands' efforts. Nevertheless, there remains such a wide gap in income levels that actual degree of improvement is more likely to be greater when husbands' incomes, and thus the family's social position, are relatively lower.

In years to come, as income differences narrow in those situations where both partners have been equally active in the labor force, class position may become less a matter of how much wives' income can improve or add to the base provided by husbands. Instead, social position may simply become the result of the combined and approximately equal inputs of each partner. In that regard, it is intriguing to observe that two future-oriented variables helped predict perceptions of current situations. It may be that some workers are anticipating increased future earnings and projecting those anticipations onto the present.

Composite Class Position

Additional clues to the mechanisms by which class position is the outcome of dual inputs are gained from another section of table 3-2. When wives responded positively to the item "positive impact of wife working on class," they were immediately asked which of the five classes that would be. From that ranking, a new variable was constructed in which household class position is based on the composite efforts of both husband and wife, and not solely on the husbands' efforts.[12]

It is of particular interest to observe that there is a significant difference ($p < .000$) between the means of the two social class scores. The mean ranking based on husbands' efforts alone is 1.97 or, in our coding scheme, just at the top of the "working class," just below the "lower-middle-class" category. But the mean score based on their composite efforts is 2.23, well into the lower-middle-class range. In short, some workers see their own efforts boosting their families into another and significantly higher social class category. The most common boost seems to be between the working class and the middle class. Given that middle-class family status is intrinsic to the "American Dream," the efforts of some workers in making that possible would seem to be an important phenomenon.

A strong influence (17 percent explained variance) on the composite social position of the household is the aggregate or combined incomes of both spouses, that is, family income. The greater the family income, the higher the family social class position. While the job statuses of each spouse are positively correlated with composite class position, neither has any predictive influence on how these wives rank their own households. The same conclusion applies to either spouse's individual income. Of greater significance than solo incomes is the dollar amount wives and husbands together are able to earn.

But, surprisingly, an even stronger predictor of composite social position is external resources. The greater the level of such skills and capabilities they have, the higher the class position at which they claim to be. The emergence of intangible resources (compare figure 2-1) to account so strongly for this particular issue is highly significant. Workers who have greater intangible resources aimed at attaining extrafamilial goals utilize these resources to increase family social position. Very likely their resources enable them to gain, hold, and advance in occupations that provide higher earnings. This effect overlaps with the three consequences of such resources discussed in connection with their support of husbands' efforts. Thus, composite (actual) family social position would seem to depend not only on the tangible resources (dollars) that working wives supply, but also ultimately on the intangible resources that wives possess in order to bring about attainment of those dollars.

Yet, it was modern sex-role preferences that showed strong effects both on family income and also on intangible resources.[13] Gender modernity (SA) also shows a direct impact on actual family position. Thus, in terms of the ongoing flow of events that have moved these families to this point on the class ladder, gender roles have over the years played a central part. Egaliatarian women have worked more frequently and also have been more "effective" in their occupations. The result has been the development of greater levels of tangible and intangible resources that, in turn, has shifted their families into a higher social position than is the case among role-traditional wives.

It is instructive to note the negative effects of 1975 family size (parity) on composite class position, whereas it bore no connection at all to husband-based class position. Workers who have more children perceive their social position to be diminished, because additional children mean that whatever economic resources they have must be stretched to fit increased demands. Therefore, overall family living standard is decreased, resulting in a lowering of perceived social position.

In addition, women with more children probably have been less active in the labor force in the past. Consequently, their current incomes probably are lower, and thus their actual contribution to composite class position is less. Recall from chapter 1 that lower 1975 parity was predicted by lower 1971 birth intentions, which in turn were predicted by modern gender preferences. Thus gender or sex roles not only have the direct and indirect effects on social position already discussed, they also have a further indirect effect via current parity.

To try to identify analogous patterns among households where wives do not work, the question was, "If you had been working, would your family's social class be different than the one based on your husband's job alone?" Unlike the lifestyle item discussed in table 3-1, here the majority (70 percent) replied negatively, while only 30 percent responded positively. Nevertheless, table 3-2 shows that their previously reported perception that "by working they would be able to increase family living standard" is, not unexpectedly, the strongest predictor of thinking that their working could also increase family social position. Peer influence on nonworkers is felt once again (compare table 3-1) since perceiving that significant others evaluate their husbands' economic provision negatively leads them to expect they could indeed contribute to class position. The same result (contribution to class position) emerges where they themselves evaluate their husbands' current occupational performance negatively (figure 2-2), and where they are gender-role-modern.

Nonworkers who responded positively to the preceding item were then asked, "Which class would that be?" A new composite class variable was constructed based on those responses using logic similar to the logic used for working wives. Hence the variable explained in the final section of table 3-2 is what wives believe their household social position would be if they were working. However, since there is no aggregate or family income within these households, husbands' own attainments remain as the most pervasive influence on projected social class. Nonetheless, wives' preferred career orientations plus 1971 TM modernity (compare figure 1-1) also positively influence their class definitions.

In brief, these data provide some additional support for the generalization indicated earlier. Namely, among nonworkers, those most concerned for their own individualistic preferences or interests are the ones who, in the long run, will probably end up contributing most to familial or household interests. In that sense, their profit-seeking (like that of workers) is likely to contribute to the maximum joint profit of all persons within their family units (Kelley and Schenitzki, 1972).

Interestingly, as was the case with workers, nonworkers report a significant ($p < .000$) increase in the mean social-class level reached solely through their husbands' efforts (1.99), and the mean level that could be reached through combined efforts (2.28). As before, the boost upwards represents a shift upward across those invisible and subtle boundaries from one class category (upper-working) to another (lower-middle).

Recap

One consequence of women's work is that it does significantly enhance family lifestyle. A second is that it likewise increases the family's social-class position as far as wives themselves are concerned. Women (both workers and nonworkers) are able to make a distinction between the position achieved solely through their husbands' efforts and the higher position actually attained (or that could be attained) by the addition of their own efforts. It is workers' own income that prompts them to make the distinction—to respond that they themselves do indeed enhance family position. And, more specifically, it is their family or aggregate income (to which they contribute significantly) that influences them in actually assigning the higher social class ranking than the one gotten solely via their husbands' inputs.

But besides the impact of these tangible resources on actual family position, there is the strong impact of intangible resources. Workers who are more skilled and capable see themselves making a greater contribution to household position. And, as with the lifestyle consequence examined earlier, sex-role preferences emerge as a pervasive force behind both the tangible and intangible resources. Just as gender-modern women bring about increased lifestyle, they also make possible higher social class rankings for their families.

But, as above, a complicating factor is that they tend to be married to gender-modern men who also earn more money. However, in the years ahead, the incomes of dual-achievers should become more or less matching. Therefore, we should be less likely to find the current inverse relationship between class position based on husbands' efforts and the impact of wife employment on family social class (table 3-2). Even when males' income and thus class position are high, if their wives are gender-modern and if they continue ever more strongly to define work as their inherent right, then they are likely to be earning comparable amounts of income that should push the family's social-class position yet higher. In short, among dual-achiever marriages of the future, there may emerge a positive relationship between the social class position that either spouse alone can gain for their household and whether the inputs of the other spouse significantly increase that position.

The relative absence of job status and the pervasiveness of income variables throughout tables 3-1 and 3-2 raise the question of which is actually the better indicator of household differentiation. This is not the place to examine that issue in detail, but in the past one reason for using husbands' job status was that it appeared to be a valid shorthand way of ranking households. And, perhaps for some purposes, it may still be valid to rank individual workers of either sex in terms of their own job status.

However, when the problem is to try to measure household social class position based on some sort of joint indicator (that, for instance, validly subsumes the lifestyle available to any children), aggregate income can be arrived at in simple fashion, and it is understood by professionals and laypersons alike. It has considerable face validity. In the minds of these respondents, for instance, income appears to be the single best indicator of class differentiation. That is probably because variations in income make possible variations in consumption patterns that, in turn, make public to other persons, at least in rough fashion, the family's social class position. The wife's dollars are tangible or hard evidence of her contribution to that public position. In any event, it is plain that ongoing changes in women's roles force examination of what actually are the most valid measures of household differentiation. Among these, I would suggest aggregate income as a foremost candidate.

Household Duties

Women believe that their paid employment increases their family's living standard and also that it does the same for the social class position of their households. The actual dollars they contribute lend "objective" credence to their convictions.

The third consequence I explore is, does wives' working have any impact on the performance of household duties? Recall from chapter 2 that behaviors can be classified as prohibitions, options, or rights. An additional category is obligation, or the inability to avoid a certain behavior or course of action. The driver must stop at a red light; the healthy male has been obligated (both by law and powerful custom) to provide for his family.

Nevertheless, the fact is that a goodly proportion of American males do not fulfill that obligation, even though the courts insist on it. Separated and/or divorced men, for instance, often do not maintain their alimony and/or child-support payments. Some men living with their families do not support them adequately, though they have the means to do so. (Other men want to provide support but cannot find jobs.)

Therefore, to assert that a duty cannot be avoided in no way guarantees that it will be carried out. What then influences persons to keep or ignore obligations? The answer is that if duties are not rewarded when fulfilled and/or punished when neglected, eventually they will cease to be fulfilled, no matter how strong or moral (Ekeh, 1975) the obligation. If that is so, is there any genuine distinction between a right and a duty? There is, because an obligation carries with it a great deal more social legitimation and stronger negative sanctions as well as positive reinforcement. That is why it is difficult (not impossible) to avoid. Others expect that it will be done; they tend to reward if it is; they will almost certainly try to punish if it is not.

A right, however, does not carry the same degree of legitimation, and thus the possibility of negative sanctions. A married woman may consider it her right to work, but if she does not exercise her right, no one is likely to punish her. Nor are American voters punished when they neglect their franchise. Furthermore, because a duty is so much more strongly institutionalized than a right, it is also surrounded by a certain aura of protection and privilege. Part of being an American police officer is the duty to apprehend alleged assailants, including the duty to shoot them if deemed necessary. In so doing, the officer is generally protected from prosecution. Similarly, the duty of providing for his family has meant that a male has been protected from incursions that might restrict his performance. Following his wife so that she can take a job elsewhere (table 2-4) has been considered one type of incursion. Household chores has been considered another.

Reference to household chores reminds us that some duties are more socially desirable and rewarded than others. It has long been considered the wife's duty to cook, sew, clean, iron, wash, and so forth. However, those duties have rarely been directly reimbursed by husbands; and when they are performed in a market situation, their pay is among the lowest available. Nevertheless, there has been strong social sanction and support for the idea that wives should perform these duties. Just as the worth of men is often judged by others on how well they perform their occupational duties, so women have often been judged (positively or negatively) by how well they perform their domestic duties. ("If your mother-in-law sees her reflection in your dinner plates, that's a nice reflection on you.")

Since among other things duty includes legitimation, support, and protection, the question is when, if ever, would it be possible to label the woman's paid employment as duty if her (healthy) husband is present? In terms of the existence of any evolution toward gender symmetry (Young and Willmott, 1973) or gender egalitarianism, it would seem that the stage at which women's work behavior becomes defined as duty is highly significant. Once the idea becomes widely held that women have the same kind of duty to be family providers as men do, that would be the signal that their work roles have become socially entrenched in the same ways that men's are. Women's work behaviors would become legitimated, surrounded, and protected by the same sort of aura that now surrounds those of the male provider. Women too would then be protected from incursions that might hinder their performance. Therefore, while movement on the continuum of work definition from option to right is extremely important, movement from right to duty (obligation) is certainly equally, if perhaps not more, important.

However, simply because both spouses recognize that duty, it does not necessarily mean that each would always work. This particular sort of obligation would not imply that one could not elect to forego it for a time should one wish to do so. The reason for that possibility is that if husband and wife are household coproviders (Scanzoni, 1972), then by definition the obligation does not fall solely on one or the other partner. Therefore, the male (as well as the female) may legitimately exit from the labor force for a period of time since she is just as responsible as he for family well-being. (Incidentally, that possibility is a benefit of emerging family changes not now legitimately open to healthy males.) But whether both are always working simultaneously or not, being coproviders does mean that extensive negotiations (and renegotiations) will have to take place between them regarding just what incursions into each other's interests will or will not be permitted. Specifically, if both spouses have the duty to provide for the household, then the husband can no longer automatically regard other duties (routine chores) as incursions. Their performance will now have to be negotiated.

Therefore, what are the conditions under which she becomes coprovider—her work, as much as his, is defined as obligation or duty? And what are the conditions that affect husband-wife performance of remaining household duties?

The Duty to Provide

To assess these kinds of issues we read the following item to our respondents: "Here are a few duties found in most families. Would you say your husband mostly does each thing, you mostly do it, or you and your husband share the duty equally?" One among several duties then read to the respondent was, "to provide for the family's financial support."

As expected, sharp and significant differences emerge when workers are separated from nonworkers. Ninety-six percent of nonworkers indicate it is the husbands' duty to provide, while less than half of workers—45 percent—so indicate. A hefty 52 percent of workers say they share it, while 3 percent claim it is mostly their duty.

In other words, some 55 percent of working women define themselves as (at least) coproviders with their spouses. They believe it is their duty to provide, just as much as it is their husbands' duty. By any token, it seems impressive that the majority of working wives consider their occupational endeavors not only their right, but also their obligation. Very likely, this proportion is greater than it was ten or twenty-five years ago. Accordingly, it is likely to increase in the years ahead.

The next question then becomes: what conditions, besides being in the labor force, help explain why some working women occupy the status of coprovider? The first section of table 3-3 displays those variables that account for shared provider duties. The strongest determinant by far is workers' own income level.[14] The more dollars they earn, the more strongly they respond that they share those provider obligations equally with their husbands. Significantly, their husbands' incomes have precisely the opposite influence—the more husbands earn, the more likely wives are to respond that their husbands (not they) provide. A third predictor is the "ratio of wife-to-husband income in 1974." The higher that ratio is, or the closer wives' earnings approximate those of husbands', the more likely they are to respond in the shared duty direction.

Plainly, therefore, objective earnings are the major direct influence on either sex being labeled as family providers. The wife's absolute dollars are most important, but so is her income relative to that of her husband. The less the disparity in spouse earnings, the more she considers herself a coprovider. The less he earns, of course, the less the disparity will be, as noted earlier. During the current era of marriage transition, full-orbed egalitarianism would, in certain respects, seem more difficult to attain where husbands hold high incomes, even

Table 3-3
Influences on Shared Household Duties, for 1975 Workers

Economic Provision[a]						
				Worked 1971 and 1975		
	beta	r			beta	r
Wife's income 1974	.33	.53		Wives' income increase	.32	.49
Husband's income	−.18	−.28		1975 PHA modernity	.29	.41
1975 PHA modernity	.16	.30		Husband income	−.27	−.29
1974 Income ratio	.20	.47		External resources	.12*	.29
Social class impact of wife	.14	.39		1975 income ratio	.13*	.45
Lifestyle impact of wife	.14	.37				

$MR = .69, R^2 = .47, n = 151$ $MR = .67, R^2 = .45, n = 106$

Childcare[b]				Cooking[b]		
	beta	r			beta	r
Coprovider	.18	.25		1975 Income ratio	.23	.29
Internal resources	.19	.16		External resources	.19	.28
1975 Income ratio	.18	.24		1975 SA modernity	.14	.24
				Catholic	.13	.17

$MR = .34, R^2 = .12, n = 126$ $MR = .42, R^2 = .18, n = 151$

Dishwashing[b]				Clothes Washing[b]		
	beta	r			beta	r
1975 Income ratio	.28	.25		1975 PHA modernity	.18	.24
1975 TH modernity	.27	.26		Appreciation resource	.16	.24
Internal resources	.16	.16		Coprovider	.15	.20
				Internal resources	.13*	.20

$MR = .41, R^2 = .17, n = 150$ $MR = .37, R^2 = .14, n = 148$

Food Shopping[b]		
	beta	r
1971 TM modernity	.21	.22
1971 Economic satisfaction	.19	.21
Catholic	.14	.16

$MR = .33, R^2 = .11, n = 161$

All betas significant at .05, unless starred.

[a]Higher score = greater wife sharing.

[b]Higher score = greater husband sharing.

though such households may tend to contain persons who are most gender-role modern. However, the finding that wives' income has the single most powerful impact on sharing this duty suggests that over time as spouse's incomes (presumably) become more equalized, the phenomenon of actual coprovider households should become more common.

Not surprisingly, table 3-3 also reveals positive connections between workers' perceiving that they contribute to increased family living standards (compare table 3-1), as well as to increased class position (compare table 3-2), and being a coprovider. To contribute to lifestyle and social class increments is nontraditional female behavior, which in turn results in nontraditional female work status.

The remaining variable in the section is 1975 PHA modernity (compare figure 1-1). Wives who prefer more individualistic gratifications in the form of concessions from their husbands are, as expected, more likely to be coproviders. Moreover, recall that wives' 1974 incomes were influenced by their prior 1971 gender roles.[15] Thus it can be argued that gender-role modernity at point 1 in time (1971) contributes to coprovider marital status at point 2 (1975) via its positive stimulation on increased earnings in 1974.

This ongoing pattern is substantiated in the data which include only women who worked at both the 1971 and 1975 interviews. Now the most powerful determinant of being coprovider is their income difference between 1970 and 1974: the greater the increase in earned dollars, the more likely they are to be coproviders by 1975. And earlier we learned that sex-role preferences were the strongest among several influences that accounted for that income increase. Furthermore, 1975 PHA now has a much stronger effect than it had in the first section of table 3-3. Here it becomes more powerful even than husbands' income in accounting for their coprovider status.

Recap

Here, as earlier in the chapter, sex-role preferences exercise pervasive influence. Because egalitarian women have been more labor-force active, they have been able to gain more tangible resources. Their gender roles motivate them to want to be coproviders, to have their working be not only a right, but also a duty. They want the legitimation, support, reinforcement, and protection afforded by that sort of institutionalized pattern. (Presumably, they are also prepared for the responsibilities and costs attached to taking on the expectations attached to that duty.)

As coprovider, incursions (from spouse or children) on their work presumably become less legitimate. Coprovider wives are less vulnerable to being "forced" by varied contingencies (compare chapter 2) to exit from the labor market. They are more able to negotiate with their husbands as to what incursions or adjustments they (wives) can legitimately press on them. Furthermore, it is their tangible resources that make individualistic goal attainment possible. Apart from their tangible resources, their egalitarian goals would be out of reach. Simultaneously, apart from their gender norms or preferences, they would not have held those goals, nor achieved those resources.

Therefore, in terms of the larger question at issue—yes, past employment does have significant impact on this particular household duty. Women who have been consistently and highly involved in the labor force are able to consider their employment an obligation. Perhaps the most tangible result of their relatively ongoing involvement is their higher earnings. The consequences of those earnings is that they rank themselves alongside their husbands in what is almost certainly the core structural feature of households, namely, the provider status.

Remaining Household Duties

There has been considerable discussion in recent years of whether there are any connections between changes in the occupational statuses of married men and women and performance of various sorts of strictly domestic chores (Oakley, 1974; Glazer-Malbin, 1976; Nye, 1976). Some spokespersons take the position that simple justice demands there *should* be, particularly in those cases where wives are employed full-time outside the home. However investigations differ on the actual extent of spouse chore sharing. Some studies indicate that working wives continue to perform those chores to the same degree as nonworkers. Conversely, other studies suggest that husbands of workers do participate more than nonworkers' husbands. (See Pleck, 1979, for a literature review.)

Therefore, besides asking these women, "Whose duty is it to provide?" we also asked them whose duty it is to do six additional things: childcare, cooking, dishwashing, clothes washing, home repairs, and food shopping. Table 3-4 (top row) shows that on five of these six behaviors, significant differences emerge between workers and nonworkers: nonworkers are more likely to respond that the five behaviors are mostly their duties; they are relatively more involved in those chores than workers. On the other hand, workers are more likely to have their husbands share those tasks.

Moreover, these conclusions are supported by the percentages in table 3-4 which also consistently indicate larger proportions of husband task sharing among workers than among nonworkers. Nevertheless, what is striking in examining these percentages is that in only one of the six areas do men in either category take primary responsibility for performance of a household duty. And that is the traditional and stereotypically male chore of making repairs around the house.

Therefore, whatever changes may be occurring among younger American households with regard to domestic chore performance, they are indeed gradual though theoretically predictable. That is, in four of the five traditionally female areas, women, whether they work or not, are more likely to perform the obligations rather than men. The one exception occurs in the childcare sphere. Husbands are more willing to share childcare than other duties—particularly if their wives work. In the "male" area, men are more likely to do that chore than

Table 3-4
Mean and Percentage Differences, by Employment, in Sharing of Household Duties

		Mean Differences				
	Cooking	Childcare[a]	Dish-washing	Clothes washing	Repairs	Food shopping
Workers[b] (n = 162)	1.70	1.20	1.60	1.74	0.34	1.55
	*	*	*	*	***	**
Nonworkers (n = 233)	1.90	1.50	1.86	1.97	0.43	1.68

		Percentage Differences[c]			
		Husband	Shared	Wife	
Cooking	Workers	1	28	71	$x^2 p < .000$
	Nonworkers	0	13	87	
Childcare	Workers	2	76	22	$x^2 p < .000$
	Nonworkers	0	50	50	
Dishwashing	Workers	1	38	61	$x^2 p < .000$
	Nonworkers	0	14	86	
Clothes washing	Workers	2	22	76	$x^2 p < .000$
	Nonworkers	0	3	97	
Repairs	Workers	70	26	4	ns
	Nonworkers	63	31	6	
Food shopping	Workers	3	41	56	$x^2 p < .03$
	Nonworkers	1	29	70	

[a]On childcare, n's = 136, 227.

[b]Higher score = woman's duty; lower score = shared duty or husband's duty.

[c]For n's, see mean score comparisons.

  *$p < .000$.

  **$p < .01$.

***ns.

are women. Thus, where evolutionary change is occurring, it is more apparent among working-wife households. Yet, it is not the sort of change where formerly "female" duties suddenly become the province of husbands.

Instead workers, for reasons considered below, are apparently more able than nonworkers to negotiate their husbands into greater sharing of these obligations. Presumably, if such trends continue into the future, not only will shared task performance become more common among dual-worker households, it is possible that certain duties may become the primary responsibility of males, or else, even more likely, become non-sex-linked. Young couples may negotiate, for instance, that husbands should cook, or wash clothes, or do any of the other tasks. The tasks may no longer be defined as "female" or "male" responsibilities, but simply as neuter chores that either can perform, at any juncture, for any length of time, as negotiated on the basis of skills, preferences, occupational demands, and so forth.

Childcare. It can be argued that besides provision the most significant household duty is childcare. It is surely fraught with powerful emotional overtones given the conviction held by many parents that children are cheated or harmed if the biological mother does not care for them during infancy and preschool years. Other parents might not mind substituting biological fathers for mothers without thinking that children are harmed. Nonetheless, there seems to be continuing concern among both citizens and politicians that alternative arrangements, such as day-care centers, will have negative effects on children.

It is, therefore, of considerable interest that recent, carefully controlled studies by Jerome Kagan and colleagues, comparing children reared in quality day-care settings with children reared at home, reveal no differences in intellectual growth, social development, and ability to achieve close relationships with their mothers.[16]

Earlier I cited census data showing that preschool children are becoming less of a factor than ever before in keeping their mothers out of the labor force (Hayghe, 1975). Another census report shows that when mothers work, the most common arrangement for childcare is that "some other relative" (very often the father) looks after the child in the child's own home. "Fairly small proportions are taken outside their home for care, either to the home of a relative, to the home of someone who is unrelated to them, or to a day-care center. Thus, the use of a day-care center is the least often reported childcare arrangement in the United States" (U.S. Bureau of Census, 1976:1).

The pattern displayed in table 3-4 corroborates Census data that fathers appear to be substantially involved in childcare. Indeed, childcare emerges as the traditionally female chore in which husbands are most likely by far to share actual responsibility. Clearly, trends in American society are shifting away from the mother being physically present with her children during all their waking hours and in the direction of other kinds of childcare arrangements. Studies such as Kagan's that receive wide media dissemination should only accelerate those trends.

But what kinds of child-care arrangements will emerge? The item, "whose duty is it to see that the children are looked after?" only touches the tip of the iceberg-like study that would be required to explore these arrangements in depth. Nonetheless, it turns out that nationally the current pattern is for husbands of working wives to engage in considerable amounts of child care. Therefore, an item such as this one may be assumed to cover situations where fathers might be the actual caretakers of the child in their own homes, or else situations in which he is responsible for taking them to and fetching them from baby-sitters or other day-care arrangements.

But why do some husbands of working wives participate more or less than other husbands? Following the logic (Scanzoni, 1972) that provider status interchangeability should predict interchangeability over remaining duties, the coprovider variable explained in the first two sections of table 3-3 is used to explain the five chores of the remaining sections. In the "real world," the two types of occupational and domestic interchangeabilities have over the years undoubtedly exercised mutual feedback on one another. Nevertheless, the basic theoretical argument (compare chapter 1) is that sex-role preferences lead women to take purposive action to achieve certain goals—among these, higher incomes—which makes it possible for them to function as coproviders with their husbands. But in order to function optimally in that situation, they require husbands' participation in domestic tasks. Male participation is therefore also a preference, goal, or interest strongly held by women.

The childcare section of table 3-3 reveals that, as expected, wives who share provider duties are more likely to have husbands who fulfill childcare duties. Conversely, where wives are not coproviders, their husbands are much less likely to be co-child-caretakers. A second predictor is the wife-to-husband income-ratio variable. The greater that ratio—the closer that wives' incomes approximate husbands'—the more that childcare duties are shared. The remaining predictor supplies additional clues as to how wives get husbands to take on more responsibilities of this sort: the greater the internal resources the wife possesses, the greater the childcare sharing (compare figure 2-1).

If it is postulated that men as the dominant group traditionally have not assumed childcare responsibilities, then the subordinate group (women) must develop ways to accomplish that behavior, if they define it in their best interests to do so. Evidently, these working wives are able to draw upon both tangible and intangible resources to achieve that goal. Negotiating and bargaining skills (internal resources) are combined with incomes that are relatively close to those of their husbands, and the result is that they are able to shift them into greater childcare participation.

Furthermore, the negotiations would seem to include not only the relative-income issue, but also the social definition of that income—her status as coprovider. The more strongly she is able to bring the weight of her provider behaviors into the negotiations, the more effective a bargainer she is. For example, the wife might, in effect, argue: "Because I supply coprovider benefits, you are obligated to provide more child-care inputs." (Compare chapter 4.) Hence, with regard to long-term paths of influence, the argument is that sex-role preferences have affected income, which influences her to function as coprovider, which now induces husband childcare participation. Chapter 2 argued that sex-role preferences and external resources mutually reinforce one another, and that external resources in turn develop internal resources. Ultimately, therefore, it appears that women with stronger individualistic interests or goals are more able than others to achieve childcare interchangeability.

Cooking. However, in explaining shared cooking duties, the coprovider status has no predictive significance at all. Instead, the strongest predictor is the wife-to-husband income ratio. And this time it is external resources that are brought to bear by working wives to achieve their goal. Evidently, the combination of higher relative income and the skills necessary to do well in the outside world, make it difficult for husbands to resist wives' requests (demands?) to share culinary duties. Indeed, both here and in regard to childcare, wives' dollar production may very well make husbands define it to be in their own interests and in the best interests of the household to cooperate. The more rewarding are their wives' economic inputs, the less grudging husbands are about shared household duties. Simultaneously, wives who are more SA modern (figure 1-1) are more persistent in negotiating for equitable sharing of this particular duty.

Dishwashing. In the dishwashing category, the TH role dimension exhibits a strong positive influence on shared task performance. Workers who are more egalitarian are less likely to accept the idea that "a man's chief responsibility should be his job" (compare figure 1-1). Domestic responsibilities such as dishwashing should be important to him as well. Similarly, whatever being "head of family" means in figure 1-1, it does not imply that he can arbitrarily extricate himself from domestic responsibilities. Furthermore, the wife-to-husband income ratio again displays a strong positive impact on the sharing of this particular duty, as do internal resources.

Clothes Washing. Equally uninspiring as dishwashing, yet equally requisite, is washing clothes. The results yield a similar theoretical pattern to those of prior topics. Gender modernity and intangible resources result in a greater likelihood that males will share this particular domestic task.

Interestingly, as was the case with childcare, the section also reveals that coproviders are more likely to have husbands share in clothes washing. Why clothes washing should be analogous to childcare in this respect, and not to cooking and dishes, is not clear.

Food Shopping. Food shopping is the last of these domestic duties that have traditionally been characterized as "women's work." However, judging by the percentages in table 3-4, husbands of workers (and nonworkers) seem more willing to share food shopping than anything else besides childcare. And, as the related section of table 3-3 shows, this is the first duty where neither the income ratio, nor a wife resource variable, nor the coprovider status appears.

However, the strongest positive influence on sharing comes from the 1971 TM gender-role dimension (compare figure 1-1). Wives who were more strongly egalitarian at that earlier point in time, were subsequently more able to get their husbands to participate more fully in this domestic chore.

Repairs. Finally, table 3-5 focuses on a domestic sphere that tradition and the percentages in table 3-4 suggest has been mostly the province of males—household repairs. However, the explanation of this phenomenon is not straightforward. First of all, the more successful that women evaluate themselves in their current occupations (compare figure 2-1), the more they participate in this traditionally male chore. Greater intangible resources also predict greater wife sharing, as does 1975 sex-role modernity.

What these three variables suggest is a complete reversal of direction from five of the chore categories in table 3-3, and more like the direction indicated by coprovider duties. That is, workers who are more successful outside the home, more gender egalitarian, and who have more resources, find themselves moving into two traditionally male duties.

Workers who are less successful (lower incomes) and more sex-role-traditional appear less likely to assert themselves to enter either of those formerly male provinces.

Table 3-5 displays results for women employed at both interview points which makes it possible to show the impact of increases in their job statuses over time. The greater the increase in their 1975 over their 1971 job-status scores, the more likely they are by 1975 to share household repairs. It could be argued that

Table 3-5
Influences on Shared Household Repairs, by Employment Status[a]

			Workers		
				Employed 1971 and 1975	
	beta	r		beta	r
Occupational			Occupational		
evaluation	.20	.25	evaluation	.25	.30
Father's education	−.19	−.16	Job status increase	.24	.18
Appreciation resource	.16	.21	Appreciation resource	.23	.28
Coprovider	−.14	−.15	Father's education	−.19	−.15
1975 TH modernity	.14	.11	1975 TH modernity	.14	.17
$MR = .38, R^2 = .15, n = 161$			$MR = .48, R^2 = .23, n = 111$		

	Nonworkers (n = 231)	
	beta	r
Husband geographic mobility	.26	.24
1975 TH modernity	.17	.21
1971 Husband job status	.17	.14
Age last child, 1971	−.16	−.14
Future impact, husband job	.13	.12
$MR = .37, R^2 = .16$		

[a]Higher score = greater wife sharing; all betas significant at .05.

increases in job status, because of the greater demands on women's time and energy, would result in women being quite willing to leave household repairs to men, especially since women still remain primarily responsible for most "female" household tasks.

Nevertheless, that pattern does not seem to occur. Women who are more successful are likely to perceive themselves as more instrumental or task-oriented (Scanzoni, 1975b). Moreover, it seems to be a pervasive complaint of some married women that men procrastinate in doing the home repairs that they are "supposed" to do. (See chapter 4.)

Therefore, women who are successful, instrumental, and gender-modern are more likely to go ahead on their own and perform the repairs (often out of exasperation) that their husbands have neglected to do. Less successful and less instrumental women may feel less capable of doing the repairs effectively, and thus refrain from them. But these findings suggest that wives who already face the greatest time demands outside the home, and yet continue to retain prime responsibility for "women's" household work, are also the ones most likely to add still further time pressures by getting more involved in traditionally male repair duties. However, the consistent findings that the husbands of such wives are also the ones most likely to share in performance of other domestic duties, including childcare, tempers the situation. Being relatively less involved in traditional women's duties may make it somewhat less difficult for women workers to perform necessary household repairs.

An additional factor (table 3-5) that ameliorates pressures on workers' time and energies is their coprovider duties: the more strongly they fulfill that function, the less they share this repair duty. Apparently, they utilize their coprovider status to provide them with bargaining power to negotiate with their husbands to get them to stop procrastinating and perform necessary household repairs.

Again, it should be stressed that since all household tasks are intrinsically neuter, there is no inherent reason for women not to begin to move into this formerly male sphere. The point is that women seem to be moving into male realms more rapidly than men are moving into female spheres. The results of that inequity are not clear at the present stage of evolutionary family development. Furthermore, this household-repair item is, among nonworkers, the only one of the six duties that can be meaningfully explained.[17] Recall from table 3-4 that this was the one behavior where working and nonworking households seemed most alike. It turns out (table 3-5) that if nonworkers believe their husbands would be willing to move geographically to accommodate wives' occupational activities (compare table 2-4), they are less likely to leave household repairs solely in the male province. The same conclusion holds if they are more sex-role egalitarian. Recall that in table 2-4 gender modernity had the strongest influence on perceptions by these nonworkers that their husbands would indeed follow them if they moved to take a job. For these kinds of reasons, the same general explanation applies to both sets of households.

Women who could negotiate their husbands into following them in the fashion described are not usual nonworkers. They must be considered to be more active and assertive. If they were employed, they would presumably evaluate themselves as more occupationally successful using the same measure applied to current workers (figure 2-2). Second, they also possess higher levels of gender modernity than other nonworkers. Therefore, on both counts, it can be said that when household repairs present themselves, they tend to have confidence that they can perform them effectively, and thus they simply go ahead and do so. Less gender-modern nonworkers, and those who do not envision their husbands following them geographically, may tend to lack that kind of confidence ("mechanical gadgets are a mystery to me") and thus be less likely to perform the repairs.

Recap. It is clear first of all that women still remain primarily responsible for household tasks that have traditionally been defined as "women's work." Second, husbands do participate more in these kinds of household tasks when wives work than when they do not. Third, because workers see it in their interests to obtain greater male participation, they utilize sex-role preferences and an array of tangible and intangible resources to accomplish that goal. The degree to which men participate because they too see it in the best interests of the household (or their wives, or themselves) to do so, or because they feel coerced, could not be ascertained from these data.

Irrespective of that crucial issue, it would seem that in the future as younger women workers become increasingly gender modern, as they develop greater levels of intangible resources, and as they (presumably) earn incomes comparable to that of husbands, we would expect them to be able to negotiate their husbands into further levels of domestic task sharing.

Observations among nonworkers suggest that, apart from possession and effective utilization of resources, their husbands will not easily be moved into performance of these kinds of duties. Moreover, there is no apparent indication that nonworkers necessarily prefer substantially greater male participation (except perhaps in childcare, and that mostly because "it's healthy for children to relate to their fathers"), probably because nonworkers do not carry the demands of external occupational responsibilities.

Therefore, as with the duty to provide which was recapped previously, *women's work does have significant consequences for these remaining duties as well.* Working means that their husbands are more likely to get involved in these duties. However, women have *not* been able to get men to participate in those household duties to the same significant extent as women have been able to get themselves involved in the provider duty. Women willingly take on more responsibility for provision, and (apparently often unwillingly) more responsibility for a second male sphere—repairs. Nevertheless, for the years ahead the trend seems clear—as women continue to increase their levels of sex role modernity, together with increases in possession of tangible and nontangible resources, they are increasingly likely to involve men in routine and nonroutine (childcare) household duties. (The involvement could be actual physical performance or else being primarily responsible that some other person or agency is hired to do the task.)

Summary and Conclusions

While chapter 2 described ongoing changes in the meanings attached to the woman as worker, this chapter explored its consequences. These consequences are viewed from the standpoint of women in the sample. As far as they are concerned, their working, first of all, does significantly improve their family's living standard. Secondly, it does significantly increase their family's social class position. Finally, it does influence household duties in important ways. It permits some of them to assume the obligation of coprovider; it also enables them to get their husbands to share obligations such as childcare, cooking, and so forth. Moreover, pervading the explanations surrounding those three types of consequences were economic resources, intangible resources, and sex-role preferences.

Drawing on the version of utilitarian or reward-cost theory presented in chapter 1, the basic theme underlying chapter 2 also underlies this chapter. Women vary in their degree of preferences or goals for gender differentiation. One result of this variation is that over the years of adolescence and the early stages of marriage some women have behaved differently than others—they have exercised differing forms of purposive action. Women who want less social differentiation and more gender interchangeability have been more actively involved in the labor force (Scanzoni, 1979b). Consequently their occupational endeavors have produced a greater payoff in tangible resources (dollars earned). Concomitantly, such women have developed their intangible resources to a greater degree—those skills and capabilities that enable them to achieve valued goals in both occupational and domestic spheres.

At the stages of their married lives when we interviewed them, it is impossible to assert definitively that either sex-role preferences, tangible resources, or intangible resources is the prime "cause" of either of the remaining two factors. Instead, each currently reinforces the other two and in turn is reinforced by them. For example, while modern preferences are establishing goals, intangible resources are making goal attainment possible in the form of tangible resources. That form of goal attainment, in turn, is likely to strengthen modern preferences and develop intangible resources still further.

One of the major consequences of this three-part syndrome is that women who are high on all three elements are most able to raise their family's basic living standard substantially. In years past, presumably, few women (even those who worked) were able to achieve that kind of impact. This important social change is being stimulated by all three factors—but most directly by the tangible resources these women possess. In terms of ongoing changes into the future, we can expect that as women consistently rank even higher on the threefold syndrome, family lifestyle will come to depend more and more on the economic inputs of both spouses, and not chiefly on those of the male. The currently prevailing notion that the living standard centers about the husband's inputs is likely to diminish slowly but surely.

That consequence leads inevitably into the second. Because the husband's economic inputs were in years past central to family lifestyle, his occupation became the prime indicator of the social class position of all household members. But as the wife's inputs affect lifestyle, and as she defines work as a right, that logic becomes increasingly inadequate. Once more the threefold syndrome contributes to wives' perceptions that they themselves are indeed able to increase significantly the social class standing of their households. Moreover, there are strong connections between what these women perceive in that regard and what they believe significant others perceive.[18] Furthermore, the actual level of dollars they supply supports their contentions both here and in regard to lifestyle. In years past, it was less likely that wives' inputs enhanced social class position than it was that their inputs resulted in some small increment in lifestyle.

Currently, however, among some families at least, those inputs do seem to have that sort of positive impact on social class differentiation. Moreover, the pervasiveness of such impacts is likely to increase during the years ahead. The idea that social class position of women and children is ascribed via the male "head of household" promises to become increasingly invalid. Particularly in an era of rapidly rising inflation and other uncertain changes that may ensue, wives' tangible inputs may become defined ever more pervasively and strongly as an institutionalized means of enhancing the class position of all household members, including the male.

Finally, both of these critical consequences are intrinsically bound up with the impacts of women's work on household duties. A corollary of the prior discussion of social class impacts is that the core household duty is said to be that of provider. A major significance of that duty or status is that its occupant is protected from automatic and arbitrary incursions from routine domestic duties, along with protection from childcare duties which, of course, are not routine. In the past the provider status has been uniquely the province of males. But, once again, the threefold syndrome described above produces variation in the degree to which it remains the province of males. Women who rank high on resources, and so forth, cooccupy that status. They are coproviders alongside their husbands. One result of that shift is that they get their husbands to participate more fully in domestic chores such as childcare. Sharing remaining chores with husbands is accomplished via elements within the threefold syndrome.

This impact, like the other two, presumably was quite rare years ago. Women simply did not cooccupy the provider status. Similarly, they did not place today's demands on husbands to get them to participate in purely domestic tasks. But analogous to the other two consequences, the notion that the husband is the main household provider is apparently less pervasive today than it once was, and it will probably continue to erode gradually in predominance.

Gradual, of course, is the watchword for all three of these ongoing consequences and their implications for fundamental gender differentiation and for marital/familial structure. Nothing is happening overnight. As documented in this chapter, one of the most significant factors impeding the course of these changes is the current level of income disparity between wives and husbands. Furthermore, in 1975, 51 percent of married women with husbands present had no earnings whatsoever (U.S. Bureau of Census, 1977:116). And even among women who do work, this chapter revealed that only about half of them consider themselves coproviders with their husbands. In other words, only a minority of married women are on the "cutting edge" of the kinds of family impacts described in this chapter. But by the same token more women are making more decisive impacts than ten or twenty years ago (Hayghe, 1975). And given the evolutionary increases we may continue to expect in women's egalitarian preferences, as well as in resource possession, it is likely that ten years hence a greater proportion of women will be more extensively involved in these three (plus additional important) consequences.

Moreover, the increasing scope of these impacts, together with women's increasing propensity to define paid employment as their inherent right, must inevitably affect women's bargaining power with their husbands. That issue is pursued in chapters 4 and 5.

Notes

1. Yes = 80 percent; no = 20 percent.
2. The wife's-income variable by itself accounted for 10 percent of the explained variance.
3. This variable was described in chapter 2, note 19.
4. This variable was explained in chapter 2, note 11.
5. See note 10.
6. For an astute journalistic account of this issue, see "The Velvet Ghetto," *New York Times*, September 18, 1976, p. 19.
7. By itself, the income-increase variable explains 10 percent of the variance. SA modernity 1971 explained income increase with a beta of .37. The next strongest predictor was continuity with a beta of .14.
8. "Within the next five years, do you think *your working* will allow your family to reach a higher living standard than it would reach if you did not work?" Yes = 75 percent; no = 25 percent.

9. "There has been a lot of talk recently about social classes in the United States. If you were asked to name a social class from this card, which one does your·husband's job place you in, that is which one do you belong to *based on your husband's job alone,* the: lower class, working class, lower-middle class, upper-middle class, or upper class?" (Percentages, respectively: 2, 31, 35, 31, 1.)

10. Yes = 26 percent; no = 74 percent.

11. Wife's income explains more variance (12 percent) than any other single factor.

12. Wives who had responded "no" to the question in note 10 were assigned the class ranking based on their husbands' efforts, as in note 9.

13. See chapter 2 regarding intangible resources. Regarding family income, TW modernity 1971 was the strongest predictor, followed by education. Betas = .29, .16, respectively.

14. It accounts for 26 percent of the explained variance.

15. See chapter 2.

16. As reported in *The National Observer*, January 8, 1977, p. 7. See also *Working Woman*, November, 1976, pp. 77-80; *Human Behavior*, February, 1978, pp. 18-22.

17. That is, there simply were no significant correlations among non-workers between any of the other household chores and the array of variables available to us.

18. The correlations ranged from .50 to .70, suggesting that as far as respondents are concerned, there is a shared set of definitions regarding these socioeconomic matters. Wives' evaluations are not, apparently, idiosyncratic to themselves.

4 Issues and Strategies in Marital Conflict

Marital conflict has probably always existed to a certain degree (Lantz, 1976). However, in the decades subsequent to the Industrial Revolution, a new dimension was introduced. Women could earn incomes independent of their husbands' control. If marital conflicts became too severe, such alternative resources made it possible for women to leave those marriages and support themselves (Scanzoni, 1972).

Simply knowing that the wife had potential access to those tangible resources was bound to influence how spouses contested with each other. The situation is comparable to that between the Arab oil states and the industrial West. Before the Arabs had resources alternative to those supplied by the West, they were dependent upon what the West made available to them and could not possibly hope to contest the West in any serious fashion. Their oil discoveries changed all that. Now they had resources that enabled them to make tough demands on the West. Struggle between the West and the Arab states has become an institutionalized feature of the modern world.

In the same fashion, struggle between spouses has become an established part of modern societies. Women's long-standing battle for symmetry inevitably brings them into increasing conflict with men's efforts to maintain the favored position of males—the status quo. That theme, implicit throughout prior chapters, now needs to be made explicit.

Purposive Action

The term *purposive action* was occasionally used in earlier chapters as a convenient way to describe women's goal-seeking behavior. As described in chapter 1, Coleman (1975) uses this shorthand label to subsume a variety of approaches: utility (reward-cost) theory, equity theory, resource theory, exchange theory, and conflict theory. Basic to all these approaches is the central core of purposive action: "For a person," writes Coleman, "each state of the world has a particular utility level, where utility is that which the person seeks to maximize, through his actions." If the person is faced with several possible outcomes or events, "he takes that action which will give him the outcomes with the highest expected utility" (p. 81).

When Coleman talks about "maximizing utilities," he is emphasizing a point also made by Collins. Collins (1975:89) contends that everyone pursues his own best line of advantage according to resources available to him and to his competitors; and that social structures— whether formal organizations or informal acquaintances [or marriage] – are empirically nothing more than men [and women] meeting and communicating in certain ways. The outlooks [persons] derive from their past contacts are the subjective side of their intentions about the future. [Persons] are continually recreating social organization. Social change is what happens when the balance of resources slips one way or another so that the relations [persons] negotiate over and over again come out in changed form.

Nevertheless, not all goal seeking involves conflict. Coleman takes care to point out that a great deal of goal seeking is carried out in the form of exchange behavior. There is thus a close connection between exchange and conflict approaches, because both stress the seeking of rewards or goals.

Such an observation is not new. "For Simmel . . . conflict and exchange were simply two intimately related forms of interaction. . . . Simmel perceived that peaceful exchange is often a substitute for conflict" (Levine et al., 1976:828). Wallace (1969:31) asserts that "conflict theory may logically be considered a variety of exchange theory insofar as it pays primary attention to the exchange of acts, albeit acts defined as injurious or punishing." He, too, notes the intermingling of the two approaches in Simmel. "In exchange theory generally," writes Wallace, "interest is . . . in the exchange of any and all acts, whether beneficial or injurious, rewarding or punishing." Duke (1976:217-218) observes that both conflict and exchange perspectives begin with the "same basic assumption" that humans pursue their "own interests at the expense of others. . . . [Humans are] essentially goal-directed and active in the manipulation of [their] own life-situation in order that [they] might make it most suitable [i.e., profitable, maximize benefits, minimize costs] to [their] own requirements."

Nevertheless, Duke also points up that there have been significant differences in the applications made and the directions taken by the two perspectives. These differences become especially apparent in viewing the work of conflict theorists in the Marxian tradition at the macro level as over against theorists operating in the Simmelian tradition at a more microlevel. Collins (1975:21) approaches conflict at the microlevel when he argues that the "basic postulate" of conflict theory is "real people seeking real interests." That this fundamental postulate could likewise be applied to social exchange is self-evident.

Continuing in the same vein as Simmel, Levine, Wallace, and Coleman, Ellis (1971) contends that both exchange and conflict are variations of what he calls utilitarian theory. Exchange perspectives, he argues, are most useful when both parties or groups seek equity based on "bilateral positive reciprocity." But conflict perspectives apply, according to Ellis, when goal seeking results in attempts at coercion, exploitation, suppression, inequities, and so forth. Utilitarianism, in short, is synonymous with purposive action.

Questions about "peaceful" or equitable exchanges were not put to the women in our sample. Rather, they were asked questions about conflict–struggle or resistance against coercion, suppression, and/or inequities. Nevertheless, a great deal can be learned about exchange processes in this chapter and the one that follows. For instance, the discussion about bargaining could apply to either a fair exchange or unjust conflict. It will become clear that, although these women are currently engaging in conflict, they want it to end. They want to resolve it and bring it instead to a fair exchange.

Not only is there a yearning for resolution on the part of subordinates during conflict, at any point during ongoing fair exchanges, conflict can erupt (Scanzoni, 1972). Any time one or the other party acts unfairly, conflict replaces exchange. It is at that juncture that this chapter "cuts in" and traces women's efforts to replace the conflict.

Measures of Conflict Processes

Sprey (1972:237) suggests that researchers tap the dynamics of family conflict by asking family members to report "what happens in terms of moves and countermoves, threats and promises, aggression and appeasement." It is precisely those kinds of processes, flows, and movements—elements intrinsic to social conflict—that I shall try to capture in these pages. Figure 4-1 describes the steps to be followed. No claim is made that the strategies presented below are the only, or necessarily the most valid, means to grasp conflict processes. They are simply one means to test theoretical models (Scanzoni, 1978, 1979c) pertaining to social process, within the constraints imposed by survey-type research.

A great number of laboratory studies of exchange theory have been carried out over the years. Rubin and Brown (1975) and Chadwick-Jones (1976) have compiled exhaustive reviews of that literature. Both conclude that it is vital to begin examining goal-seeking processes outside the laboratory in the "real world." To be sure, some such attempts have already been made (Raush et al., 1974; Kantor and Lehr, 1975; LaRossa, 1977). However, with the notable exception of Straus (1976), most of the work outside the laboratory has been done on small, nonrepresentative (sometimes clinical) samples.

Since the information that follows is based on a comparatively large sample that is fairly representative of younger white married women, some confidence can be placed in the generalizability of the findings. In other words, these conflict processes (as well as patterns observed in earlier chapters) probably reflect what is going on among most younger white (and many black) American marriages—at least from the standpoint of wives.

Questions about conflict were read to respondents in sequence, much as portrayed in figure 4-1. In reality, of course, that neat progression is complicated by many factors. First, these processes may often occur simultaneously. (As discussed later, conflict and power are actually interlocked, as is bargaining

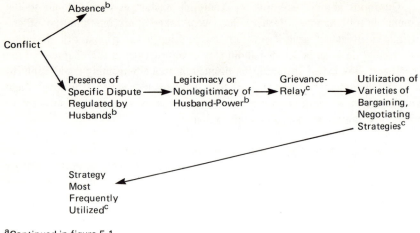

^aContinued in figure 5-1.

^bAs perceived by wives.

^cWives' reported behavior.

Figure 4-1. Ongoing Progression of Processes in which Husbands Are Attempting to Maintain Regulation of Conflict and Wives Are Attempting to Replace That with a Fair Exchange[a]

power.) Or they may occur in a different order from that portrayed in the figure. Furthermore, while respondents were answering questions with reference to one particular issue (for example, money), several interrelated issues may have been involved—especially in the striking of bargains. ("If you 'let' me go to work, I won't spend so much of *your* money.")

As always, however, the scientist must abstract out from total reality those particular elements in need of intensive investigation. To do so inevitably runs the risk of oversimplification. Nevertheless, although the high degree of inherent complexity in the case at hand needs to be recognized, it is hoped that the techniques described below will permit a degree of understanding and insight that has heretofore escaped investigators.

Regulated Conflict

Some conflicts in marriage are resolved; in other cases, the issues are never fully cleared up in a way satisfactory to both partners. To discover such occurrences, we read the following to each respondent:

> In every marriage there are things a wife wishes her husband would do or stop doing. For example, they might want their husbands to stop

spending so much time with his friends or at work. Some wives want their husbands to spend more money for family needs, some want them to stop spending so much money. Some want their husbands to discipline the children more, some want them to stop being too hard on the children. Some wives want their husbands to let them work or let them visit their family more often. Other wives wish their husband would cooperate so they could have the number of children they want. Thinking about your situation, *what is the one most important thing your husband should do or stop doing?* (Probe: *Exactly* what would you like him to do or stop doing?)

The sequence begins by allowing the respondent to name the area of disagreement or conflict that is most significant to her. The issue is something that currently keeps (or else very recently kept) surfacing between her and her spouse so that it comes to mind when queried by the interviewer. If at some sufficiently remote point in the past they had stopped disagreeing about some particular matter, it would then no longer be salient enough to report. It may be said that such conflicts had actually been resolved or, as Sprey (1971) puts it, "made to go away." But both Sprey and Dahrendorf (1959) call attention to the critical distinction between conflict that is resolved (becomes replaced by a fair exchange) and conflict that simply persists (that is, regulated conflict).

Modifying Coser (1956), conflict can be defined as "Actor's struggle against Other's resistance towards Actor's efforts to achieve intended goals." For example, Actor's goal is to enter the labor force. Other (husband) refuses to "let" her do so, and she struggles with him to bring that goal about. That is regulated conflict in the sense that one partner has enough power to subvert the other's aims, keep the conflict from being resolved, and protract the struggle indefinitely.

Absence of Regulated Conflict

In spite of the fact that the item read to respondents began with the words, "in *every* marriage," some wives (14 percent) were unable to name anything that they wished their husbands "would do or stop doing." Of this number almost half supplied instructive comments. "No problem; you see, if I want something or want to go someplace, I just ask him. If he says 'OK,' we go; if he says 'no,' we don't." At the opposite pole: "I make all the decisions. He agrees; so I have no complaints." Somewhere in between: "I don't know. We both do our own things—he does what he wants and I do what I want, and we don't have any problems."

The comments of some wives gave indication of conflicts in the past that had been resolved. An example of such a statement is this one: "Nothing. Since I'm not working, everything is fine." The comments of other wives simply indicated great enthusiasm over their husbands' behaviors: "I can't answer that.

We get along terrifically. I don't think he can do any more than he's done for us." "There is nothing I would change; we have a very good arrangement together. He is a very cooperative husband and father." "I am completely satisfied. We do things together, and he's interested in the family." "I hate to say he's perfect, but there is nothing I would change. He's fantastic!"

To account for the absence of regulated conflict, a variable was devised in which women with no reported disagreement were contrasted with those who reported some contested issue. Table 4-1 reports the results separately for 1975 workers and nonworkers.[1]

Table 4-1

Influences on Presence of Regulated Conflict, Husband Fairness, and Wife Grievance-Relay, by Employment Status

Workers (n = 162)			Nonworkers (n = 232)		
Is Regulated Conflict Present? (Positive Score = No)					
	beta	*r*		*beta*	*r*
1975 Empathy	+.24	.27	1975 TH Modernity	−.20	−.22
Budget skills	+.22	.24	Worked since marriage	−.14	−.17
Some 1970 income	−.14	−.13	Current aspirations		
Occupational evaluation	+.12	.18	for husband	−.16	−.15
1975 Births desired	+.15	.17	1975 Empathy	+.15	.13
Social class-husband	+.12	.17	Looking for a job	−.12	−.12
$MR = .45, R^2 = .20$			$MR = .36, R^2 = .13$		
Is Husband Fair? (Positive Score = Yes)					
	beta	*r*		*beta*	*r*
1975 Empathy	+.24	.33	1975 Empathy	+.20	.25
Job satisfaction	+.23	.23	1975 Economic		
Job expectations			satisfaction	+.13	.23
for husband	+.16	.20	Conflict-peer, kin	−.16	−.19
Wife impact on future			Budget skills	+.14	.17
living standard	−.15	−.20	Looking for a job	−.14	−.14
Wife shares repairs	−.13	−.17			
Conflict-children	−.12	−.17			
$MR = .49, R^2 = .24, n = 140$			$MR = .40, R^2 = .15, n = 195$		
Can Wife Relay Grievance? (Positive Score = Yes)					
	beta	*r*		*beta*	*r*
Conflict-economic	−.32	−.30	1975 Companionship	+.22	.24
Wife shares repairs	−.22	−.24	Husband shares dish-		
1975 Empathy	+.20	.21	washing	+.14	.16
Job satisfaction	+.15	.14	Coital frequency	+.11	.15
$MR = .46, R^2 = .21, n = 140$			$MR = .30, R^2 = .09, n = 193$		

All betas significant at .05.

Employed Women and the Absence of Regulated Conflict

Among workers, the strongest influence on conflict absence is their 1975 empathy satisfaction.[2] The more positive the empathy satisfaction, the less is the likelihood of any ongoing disagreement. Apparently, more effective empathy enables workers to resolve conflicts so that the conflicts do not become institutionalized (regulated). Almost certainly these employed wives have experienced past disagreements with their husbands—even struggles and resistance. But evidently they have been able to negotiate fair exchanges. The impact of empathy is not surprising. It follows logically that workers who experience more satisfactory communication and understanding from their husbands are therefore more likely to be able to apply those processes to the resolution of resistances and struggles.

Elsewhere I reported that empathy was positively influenced by satisfaction with husbands' economic provision (Scanzoni, 1975a). Thus, greater objective resources provided by husbands tend to reduce the existence of regulated conflict. One reason is that higher-status husbands have greater amounts of tangible resources with which to bargain. Wives therefore may be willing to settle disputes more quickly because of their husbands' ability to supply greater inducements to do so.

Several additional factors also predict conflict absence among employed wives, with the resource of greater skill in budget management[3] ranking second to empathy. The positive impact of budget skills is also not surprising. As cited later, the literature indicates that socioeconomic issues appear to be the most common type of ongoing household conflict. The ability to skillfully manage finite economic resources is in itself an intangible resource, and women who possess it are more likely to be able to resolve the numerous economic issues that inevitably arise within all households. Quite possibly, part of this particular management skill is the capability of negotiating effectively with husbands in the event of clashes over consumption choices. Empathy facilitates that type of negotiation; and in conjunction with wives' management skills, the outcome is more frequent conflict resolution.

Nonemployed Women and the Absence of Regulated Conflict

Among nonworkers, the pattern shifts somewhat because the most powerful influence on conflict resolution is TH 1975 (See figure 1-1). Nonworkers who are more gender-role-traditional are more likely to report past resolutions (thus, conflict absence). Nonworkers who are more egalitarian, however, tend to report current regulated conflicts.

The explanation would seem to be this: Wives who adhere to the long-standing "patriarchal ideology" are less likely to dispute with their husbands. Since there is no struggle or resistance, there is no conflict. In cases where such a wife does dispute with her husband, she is more likely simply to accept the arrangements he prescribes in order to settle the issue in question. Conversely, wives who are more dubious of male prerogatives are more likely to enter into conflict with their husbands. And they are less likely to accept as just the settlements husbands propose. Such wives may be more likely to perceive that their husbands often seek settlements based on long-standing male privileges rather than arrangements that are beneficial to wives as well.

This specific pattern is indicative of the more general struggle between subordinate and dominant groups. Among women who accept the status quo, there is less tendency to actually keep on challenging male-generated arrangements. But among women who question the status quo, male-generated arrangements are continually being challenged. Hence, regulated conflict is more likely to occur.

Reinforcing this pattern is the fact of a wife's ever having worked for pay since marriage. Wives who have been employed are more likely to report ongoing conflict; those who have not been employed do not report regulated conflicts. Similarly, nonworkers who report that they are currently seeking employment are also more likely to report the presence of regulated conflicts. Perhaps the job seeking itself becomes a contention in those households, along with the desire for wife-autonomy it may tend to indicate.

Furthermore, wives who hold higher occupational aspirations (figure 2-2) for their husbands are also more likely to report conflicts. As noted below, wanting husbands to "do better" in their jobs is one type of ongoing conflict reported by some wives. Finally, the impact of empathy is, in the case of nonworkers, similar to that described for workers.

Categories of Conflicts

Among wives reporting some issue with their husbands, there were seven categories of conflict.

Socioeconomic

The largest single category (23.4 percent) was "socioeconomic," a finding borne out by earlier studies (Scanzoni and Scanzoni, 1976:337). Areas subsumed within this category include such matters as: the husband is not doing well enough on his job in terms of adequate economic provision; the husband spends too much money; the husband is too miserly and tightfisted; the husband attends so much to his work that he does not attend to his family; and so forth. Sample comments: "He should go back to school so he can get a better job." "I would like him to make more money." "Get a better job; he can do better."

"Stop spending so much money." "Doesn't realize the cost of living." "Spend more money on the house—furnishings and repairs." "Stop working so much." "Preoccupation with job . . . interferes with home life."

Peer/Kin Relations

The second largest reported set of conflicts was peer/kin relations (22.6 percent). In this category appeared comments such as: "I wish my husband would grow up . . . stop wanting other women." "Stop going to his mother's all the time." "Let me visit my family more." "Should let me entertain more." "Stop being with his friends so much . . . leaves me sitting home." "Spend more time with our kids instead of his own folks."

Child-related Issues

Third on the list of categories of conflict were child-related issues (14.9 percent), and these items centered mainly around two opposite complaints. Some wives reported that their husbands discipline the children too often and/or too harshly ("Spends more time yelling at the children than showing affection." "I think he's too rough on the boys . . . expects too much from them."). Other wives reported that their husbands do not discipline often enough and/or too mildly ("Not be so lenient with kids. He's a pushover with kids." "If kids need a spanking, it's up to mother.").

Husbands' Household-Task Performance

Wives' complaints of husbands' failures to fulfill wives' expectations regarding household-task performance comprised the fourth category (12.0 percent). These tasks include those discussed in chapter 3, plus others such as lawn and yard work. The major complaint is male procrastination and occasionally outright neglect. Typical comments were these: "Doing his chores without being nagged by me." "If I weren't pregnant, I'd get out and do it myself." "Wish he would . . . fix my car." "Just get things done around the house . . . he puts off too much. . . . in football season, it's football first." "Help around the house more—regular housework."

Socioemotional Issues

The fifth category of conflict dealt with expressive or socioemotional issues between wives and husbands (7.6 percent). Wives commented as follows: "Show more consideration for me and desire more companionship with me." "I wish he would be more attentive and show affection." "He should give more nonsexual touching." "I'd like him to be more supportive of me when I need help." "I wish he'd stop wanting more sexual response than I am capable of." "I wish he would be more open with me about his problems." "I'd like for him to try to understand my emotional needs." "I'd like him to be able to sit down and talk things out more than we do—he's not much of a talker." "Huge lack of compassion."

Wife-Autonomy

A sixth category (3.8 percent) deals with issues surrounding wife-autonomy and independence. This category, more than any of the others, contains the most explicit expressions of preferences for egalitarianism. While preferences for female rights and privileges are clearly present in the other categories, they are implicit. Here they are open and pronounced: "He should stop being threatened by my growth as an individual. . . . I'm changing beliefs that we have had since we were married. . . . I'd like to pursue things I'm interested in. . . . I'd like to pursue the idea of working . . . being a counselor . . . and he is not supportive . . . of my thinking." "He does not encourage and support me enough in the things I want to do, my own personal things, like go into nursing training. . . . He couldn't care less whether I went into it or not." "He feels that men have more rights than a woman. . . . I've got him out of it a little bit . . . because I work now." "I'd like him to leave me by myself so I can pursue my own interests." "I want him to let me work ` . . . just to get out of the house." "He should stop thinking I should be here with him every minute he's home." "He treats me like a child. . . . He tries to tell me what to wear and what to do." (See also chapter 1, p. 18.)

Miscellaneous Areas of Conflict

In addition to the six areas of conflict just described, a number of items were clustered together and labeled "miscellaneous" (15.8 percent). This category included a variety of wives' personal complaints about shortcomings of husbands and the annoyance wives felt in view of such shortcomings. Typical examples: "Stop being so passive about things." "Stick up for himself more." "Have more patience." "I wish he wouldn't be so short-tempered." "I wish he were more outgoing." "Change his appearance—I hate the way he looks." "Get more physical exercise; he's out of shape and overweight." "Take preventive action to protect his health." "More understanding to other people—such as long-haired hippies or young black teenagers."

Legitimacy of Husbands' Power

After naming the most important thing they wished their husbands would do or stop doing, the respondents were asked: "Now think about this matter, about what he does or doesn't do, about what he says and feels. Do you, personally, think that it is *fair* to you that he is this way?" As expected, a large majority (69 percent) of wives replied in the negative. While another 9 percent were unsure, a sizeable 22 percent thought it was fair.

Why these differences? Table 4-1 presents those variables that explain perceived justice. Among both workers and nonworkers, empathy exercises the strongest positive influence on perceived fairness. Thus, irrespective of a regulated conflict, empathy has the effect of influencing wives to discount inequity and injustice and to respond that, in spite of resistance and struggle with their spouses, their husbands' behavior is not necessarily unfair.

Apparently, processes of communication and understanding make it possible for some wives to take the role of the other, to put themselves in their spouses' position and simply understand their husbands' interests. Therefore, this *verstehen* enables them to see the fairness that their husbands themselves ascribe to their position. But at the same time, these wives see the justice in their own position. Had they been asked if their own position were unfair, their reply would quite surely have been in the negative. Some wives, then, seem to see justice in both positions; therefore, they are unwilling to characterize the opposition as necessarily unfair.

One might suspect that the particular conflict issue would also have some impact on perceived justice or injustice. The data reveal that, among workers, if the conflict is over children (see specific content noted earlier), the women are more likely to respond that their husbands' resistance is unfair. Among nonworkers, those who identify the conflict as peer/kin or who may be facing conflict over their current job seeking are also more likely to define their husbands' behavior as unjust. In short, it is not merely empathy by itself that affects perceptions of justice, but the issue over which resistance and struggle are occurring.

Economic Provision and Legitimacy of
Husbands' Power

Recall that empathy is generated by husbands' economic provision. That provision becomes a resource whereby husbands may be said to "purchase" definitions of justice. The better that husbands provide, the more hesitant are wives to judge their husbands as unfair or to think that husbands do not deserve the rights they assume. The likelihood of this path of influence is reinforced by nonworkers' 1975 economic satisfactions: the more positive these satisfactions are, the more probable it is that wives think their husbands are acting justly.[4]

At least since Max Weber, a distinction has been made between legitimate and nonlegitimate power (Bendix, 1962). The term *legitimate* refers to exercise of power that is just and reasonable as defined by the power-recipient (Blau, 1964). Legitimate power has also been called *authority*. Blau, among others, suggests that authority is ascribed by B to A in accordance with the overall benefits provided by A to B. In other words, power recipients are willing to call their conformity "fair" if they receive enough rewards in return.

Looking back on the wording of the item that tapped conflict regulation, it seems that husbands are by definition currently exercising more power than wives over this dispute. Analytically, it is possible to distinguish conflict from power. For example, conflict was defined above as "struggle against resistance." Power has been defined as the "capability to achieve goals despite resistance." However, the obvious connection between those definitions underscores Duke's (1976) argument that conflict does not exist apart from power, although power may occur without conflict being present. Conflict persists because each side possesses sufficient power to pursue its own interests. If one party or the other had enough power to stop the other's conflict-producing behavior, the dispute would be terminated. Here, for instance, if wives had sufficient power to attain their goal of changing their husbands' behavior, the reported issues would no longer remain as disputes. At the same time, neither do husbands possess enough power to attain their presumed goal of stopping their wives' efforts to change them.

Thus, power is more accurately "balance of power." It is inextricably tied to the dispute or conflict; and here, in any case, the balance is tipped in husbands' favor. The husbands are accomplishing their goal of persisting in their current behaviors in the face of their wives' resistance. If those arguments are granted, then it is not difficult to accept the additional point that what is being measured in the middle row of table 4-1 is the legitimacy of that power. Opponent is able to control (regulate) a conflict situation, that is, maintain the status quo. If that control is deemed fair, then Opponent exercises legitimate power; if Opponent is unfair in his (or her) control, then the power is nonlegitimate. And the legitimacy of power is based on resources supplied.

Therefore, to refine the above and perhaps somewhat crass suggestion that husbands "purchase" justice, it may be said that greater resources supply husbands with greater legitimated power. The argument is further reinforced by the finding that the greater the expectation that their husbands will actually attain higher occupational levels (compare figure 2-2), the more likely workers are to respond that their husbands are "fair."

Grievance-Relay

When actors or groups define situations or arrangements as against their own best interests, an important consideration is whether or not they are able to relay their grievances to their opponent. When feelings of injustice and nonlegitimate power are assigned to these grievances, are they able to communicate the perceived inequities? By use of the term *communicate*, such notions of relay are all that are meant. What is *not* implied is any notion that "communication solves everything" and that relaying grievances and/or perceived injustice will by itself resolve the conflict (Brickman, 1974). When asked, "Are you able to tell your husband your opinion about the way he is in this matter?" 93 percent of wives reporting some regulated conflict said they could tell their husbands. This finding should put to rest any notion that relay by itself will resolve an actual clash of interests. What, then, are some of the factors associated with a wife's reporting that she is able or unable to express her grievances to her husband, including telling him when she thinks he is being unfair?

Employed Women and Grievance-Relay

Among workers, it turns out that a particular conflict area (socioeconomic issues) shows the strongest influence. If the regulated conflict is over issues related to money, these wives report that they are less likely to be able to relay grievances to their husbands than if the conflict is over something else. Furthermore, wives who share more fully in household repairs (see table 3-5) are less able to communicate grievances. Linking that finding with the fairness question just discussed, it would appear that not only do workers consider repair sharing unfair; some find it difficult to tell that to their husbands.

In short, two kinds of matters—socioeconomic and repair-sharing—seem most likely to impede employed wives' efforts to try to resolve them via discussion. It may be that, on these particular disputes, husbands are most adamant in their refusal to change. Nevertheless, greater empathy and job satisfaction simultaneously predict more effective communication.

Nonemployed Women and Grievance-Relay

Positive companionship[5] is the strongest predictor of grievance-relay among nonworkers. Evidently, "doing things together during leisure time" enables these wives to communicate grievances and injustices. Those with less satisfactory companionate behaviors find that task more difficult, as do wives with lower coital frequency[6] and wives whose husbands do not share in the dishwashing chore (described in chapter 3). Therefore, while for the great majority of women grievance-relay does occur, it is insightful to learn that positive companionship provides a situational context that facilitates the communication of regulated conflicts.

Bargaining and Negotiation

Thus far, the presence of regulated conflicts has been established, along with the conditions under which they are defined as just or unjust. It also became clear that the majority of wives are able, at least to some degree, to relay to their husbands their definition of the conflict situations. Now the question is, what was the content of those communications? It is assumed that a large segment of those grievance-relays consists of attempts to negotiate or bargain with their husbands to resolve the conflict—to move from regulation to resolution or, in other words, to change the patterns that currently envelop them.[7]

Given those assumptions, the next item was as follows:

> On this card are a list of reasons you might give your husband to try to change him on this matter, and make him see things your way. Which of these reasons do you give him? Please give me the letters of all the reasons you use.
> A. He should because I do so much for him.
> B. He should because then I'll do something he wants.
> C. He should because it's the best for the entire family.
> D. He should because it's only right and fair.
> E. He should because it's his responsibility.
> *F. Some other reason:
>   1. Husband's own best interests.
>   2. Wife's own best interests.
>
> *(Item "F" was open-ended, and the reasons supplied by respondents were coded as F-1 and F-2.)

These statements represent arguments, reasons, rationales, and strategies that wives might use to try to persuade their husbands to change their behavior relative to the particular regulated conflicts that exist between them. More than one bargaining strategy could be stated, and the most frequent strategy reported was C ("He should because it's best for the entire family."), with 67.7 percent of respondents who reported strategies naming this one.[8] Next in line was D, with 42.2 percent reporting that they utilized the rationale that "he should because it's only right and fair." The argument that a husband should change a particular behavior "because it's his responsibility" (E) was used by 29.5 percent. Strategy A ("He should because I do so much for him.") was named by 11.6 percent. And close behind it (with 11.3 percent) was an answer volunteered by respondents in reply to the open-ended category: "He should because it's in my (the wife's) best interests" (F-2). Another strategy volunteered by respondents and used by 8.5 percent was F-1 in which it was argued that the change would be in the husband's own best interests. Used least of all was bargaining strategy B; only 6.8 offered the rationale that "he should because then I'll do something he wants." Let us examine each of these in turn.

Group Interests (Strategy C)

The most widely used strategy, C ("He should because it's best for the entire family"), is essentially an appeal to change based explicitly on collective well-being. In this case, it is the profit of the entire family group and not just that of the particular actor who presses the dispute. Such arguments, therefore, carry with them strong overtones of "moral obligation" in the senses described by Ekeh (1974)—especially if the interests of children (who are innocent to the dispute) are invoked. The wife is able to negotiate with her husband that he should change because it is best for the children, the marriage, and the family as a whole.

To explain further the choice of bargaining strategy C, consider the related sections of table 4-2.

Employed Women and the Use of Strategy C. The more children (parity) workers have, the more likely they are to negotiate with their husbands on the basis of group or familistic interests.[9] Recall from chapter 1 that 1975 family size was predicted strongly by 1971 birth intentions, which in turn were predicted best by gender roles.

Gender-role-traditional women want more children because children are a source of time-honored conventional female gratifications. Several years later, it turns out that they do in fact have more children. And the presence of children becomes a highly significant element in affecting the kind of bargaining strategy these wives use to try to resolve conflict. These women use arguments that take into account the entire family unit, including those larger numbers of children.

Furthermore, regulated conflict over children turns out to be a second predictor of the use of bargaining strategy C. There is a connection ($r = .17$) between parity and child-conflict, suggesting that the more children women have, the more likely they are to have disagreements with spouses over child-discipline. And the means chosen to try to resolve those disputes is basically group-oriented rather than individualistic—hence, the use of strategy C.

A variable that is even more robust in explaining use of this strategy is the 1971 TM role dimension (compare figure 1-1). The more traditional these wives were on this 1971 dimension, the more likely they are in 1975 to utilize a familistic bargaining strategy. Conversely, gender-role-modern wives are less likely to employ that type of strategy. Whereas gender-traditional women want their husbands to change behaviors so that the unit as a whole would profit, women who are more gender-modern (and better-educated) tend not to negotiate that way. Preferring more individualistic gratifications, they tend to choose other grounds on which to bargain with their husbands instead of relying on bargaining strategies that primarily promote the well-being of the unit qua unit.

This divergence in strategy cannot be isolated from the finding that

Table 4-2
Influences on Choice of Bargaining Strategies C, D, E, A,
by Employment Status

Workers			*Nonworkers*		
		Is Strategy C Used?[a]			
	beta	r		beta	r
1975 Parity	+.20	.28	Conflict-autonomy	−.27	−.29
1971 TM modernity	−.23	−.26	Conflict-children	+.18	.23
Conflict-economic	+.30	.23	Worked, 1971	+.15	.22
Conflict-children	+.18	.18	Husband fair	−.17	−.18
Education	−.16	−.26	Marriage-age	+.19	.15
1975 Empathy	−.14	−.20	Conflict-expressive	−.18	−.15
			Conflict-chores	−.14	−.16
			1975 Empathy	−.13	−.15

$MR = .53, R^2 = .28, n = 137$ $MR = .53, R^2 = .28, n = 184$

Workers			*Nonworkers*		
		Is Strategy D Used?[a]			
	beta	r		beta	r
Husband fair	−.16	−.22	1975 TW modernity	+.19	.21
Wife responsible			Husband shares		
for cooking	+.15	.22	clothes washing	+.19	.18
Husband education	−.20	−.22	1975 Birth		
Age last child,			intentions	−.17	−.18
1971	+.20	.12	Conflict-economic	−.14	−.15
Occupational					
expectations	−.17	−.21			
Husband mobility	−.16	−.18			
Conflict-autonomy	+.13	.13			

$MR = .46, R^2 = .22, n = 136$ $MR = .35, R^2 = .12, n = 184$

Workers			*Nonworkers*		
		Is Strategy E Used?[a]			
	beta	r		beta	r
1975 SA modernity	−.25	−.25	Conflict-chores	+.30	.31
Conflict-chores	+.17	.25	Continuity	+.15	.10
Social class-			Optimistic re		
husband	−.15	−.21	future living		
Conflict-			standard	−.14	−.21
expressive	−.17	−.18	Husband-fair	−.10	−.13
Conflict-economic	−.16	−.17			

$MR = .46, R^2 = .21, n = 137$ $MR = .39, R^2 = .15, n = 184$

Table 4-2 continued

Workers				Nonworkers		
			Is Strategy A Used?[a]			
	beta	r			beta	r
Conflict-chores	+.21	.21		Husband mobility	−.17	−.20
Conflict-autonomy	+.19	.18		1975 Empathy	−.11*	−.18
1971 Birth				Conflict-chores	+.15	.12
intentions	−.15	−.18		1971 Children		
Wife impact-				wanted	−.13	−.14
social class	+.14	.18		1975 Companionship	−.12	−.17
$MR = .36, R^2 = .13, n = 137$				$MR = .33, R^2 = .11, n = 184$		

All betas significant at .05, unless starred.
[a]Positive score = yes.

gender-traditional women have more children. Nor can it be divorced from a second specific conflict issue that emerges, namely, that women who are experiencing conflict with spouses over socioeconomic issues are more likely to use these familistic bargaining strategies than are those who encounter other types of disputes. Earlier reports (Scanzoni, 1975b) provide evidence that women who have more children report lower economic satisfactions. Apparently, some of these women express their economic dissatisfactions to their husbands, thereby generating conflict with them over socioeconomic issues. To try to resolve the conflict, the wives then utilize negotiating stance C. Thus, having more children by itself gives rise to that kind of bargaining; and, in addition, children also exacerbate economic dissatisfactions that lead to conflicts in which such bargaining strategies are utilized.

Finally, employed wives whose empathy satisfaction is low also resort to this particular strategy. It is likely that poor empathy has this effect because it is correlated with higher parity, or greater numbers of children.[10]

Nonemployed Women and the Use of Strategy C. In the related section of table 4-2, four different conflict issues predict use of strategy C, the most powerful of these being the wife-autonomy issue. Nonworkers who report that their own autonomy and independence is the chief issue currently in dispute with their husbands tend *not* to use appeals to group well-being to try to resolve it. Instead they opt for alternative strategies. Getting their husbands to change regarding the autonomy issue is not something that can easily be argued from a group-oriented stance. Indeed, such changes could conceivably have long-range negative consequences for system stability, since the consequences of greater individualistic freedom are never wholly predictable.

Simultaneously, nonworkers who report expressive and household chore conflicts also tend not to opt for strategy C. The explanation is analogous to the autonomy issue. Apparently, it is not so much group well-being that is at stake in these two conflict areas as it is the well-being of the woman herself. These women do not utilize familistic strategies to achieve greater expressive inputs or household task inputs from their husbands. As with autonomy, they opt for other bargaining bases. On the other hand, when it comes to the matter of conflict over child-discipline, nonworkers resort to strategy C just as workers do.

Fairness (Strategy D)

In an article in the popular press, Pogrebin (1977:44) writes: "Only emotional empathy, decency, and a sense of fairness can motivate a man's desire to change. So you try a consciousness-raising exercise." Evidently such reasoning also appealed to many women in our sample, since 42.2 percent reported the use of bargaining techniques based explicitly on arguments of fairness, equity, and justice.

Strategy D (table 4-2) is in some ways similar to Strategy A (ongoing benefits) discussed below. When wives argue that they themselves have already made significant inputs into their husbands, might it not be expected that they would be convinced that changes in their husbands' behavior would be only right and fair? That is the sort of theoretical argument often found in the literature (Homans, 1974; Blau, 1964).

But while both strategy D and strategy A may be based on obligations generated by past inputs, the nature or type of obligation may differ. Both Ekeh (1974) and Heath (1976) point out that obligations can either be specific and concrete or else general and diffuse. For instance, when wives say, "He should change because I do so much for him" (A), they may have in mind specific, tit-for-tat exchanges. There is a *quid pro quo* that is fixed in their minds. "Since I encouraged him to get ahead in his occupation, he should now do the same for me." "I cooked dinner all those years, now let him cook for a while."

In contrast to those specific deals, wives may also sense a kind of diffuse reciprocity owed them by their husbands. Strategy D may reflect that more generalized orientation, with no specific tit-for-tat or *quid pro quo* in view. It is simply that since marriage these wives have, as a fundamental principle, "done their duties," and thus have been "right and fair" to their husbands. In return, they expect their husbands to reciprocate—to act on the basis of this same general yet fundamental principle of rightness and fairness. This may be something of what Pogrebin has in mind in the suggestion of a "consciousness-raising exercise" that appeals to a husband's sense of fairness. Part of such an exercise would be to have the husband imagine himself living with a roommate. "Would he dump all the drudgework on his buddy?" Pogrebin asks (1977:44).

Among the nonemployed women in our sample, there is explicit evidence that gender-role preferences are related to the utilization of the fairness strategy. Nonworkers who are more gender-traditional tend not to opt for it; those who are more gender-modern employ it. Very likely, their modernity tends to stimulate the conviction that they have indeed made many contributions to their association over the years without necessarily expecting any specific rewards in return. Consequently, they now feel they can draw on that fundamental commitment to the relationship in order to negotiate changes from their husbands.

As in the case of strategy C, gender-role preferences are shown to have a direct impact on choice of bargaining strategy. The data for strategy C showed that gender modernity militated against the choice of the extreme collectivist or group-oriented strategy. It is not surprising therefore that here in the strategy E section modernity tends to stimulate selection of a comparatively less collective and somewhat more individualistic approach to bargaining.

Duty (Strategy E)

Strategy E is an appeal to duty. The wife expects the husband to behave in a certain fashion primarily because he has been assigned certain responsibilities or obligations. Whether the wife developed these expectations out of past negotiations in which the husband agreed to settle earlier disputes by performing these obligations, or whether she holds them as part of prevailing norms regarding male behaviors, current negotiations are based on the premise that "you are responsible to do it."

Considerable light is shed on the dynamics of the strategy by observing that the dispute that influences its use centers around household chores (table 4-2). Evidently, these chores are the kinds of behaviors that both workers and nonworkers single out when they choose this technique. Furthermore, the data reveal that women married to lower-status husbands are more likely to employ this strategy. It seems that wives of men who make fewer economic inputs into the household expect them to compensate by making greater chore inputs. In other words, if these husbands do not perform up to wives' expectations in the external milieu, they then are responsible to meet wives' expectations for increased performance in their internal milieu. Or the explanation may be that, while wives' expectations are constant across social strata, lower-status men are more resistant to participation in what they consider "women's work."

Among workers, it is particularly intriguing to find that women who are more gender-modern are not likely to resort to this strategy. This finding may in part be the result of such women being married to higher-status men, thus making it less necessary (for reasons just discussed) for them to employ this theme. The other side of the coin is that role-innovative women are, as observed in chapter 3, more likely to be able to negotiate their husbands into performance of traditionally female household tasks. The result is to undercut the presence of chore-related disputes in general, which likewise undercuts the tendency to resort to the duty theme.

Among nonworkers, the more months they had worked during the 1971-1975 time interval (continuity), the more strategy E is used. Although these women are not currently working, it may be that when they were employed, their husbands assumed certain chores, only to relinquish them once again when the wives ceased to work. Among women who were employed for a longer period of time, these help-patterns of husbands may have become more or less expected, that is, male responsibilities. This explains in part such wives' reliance on strategy E to overcome their husbands' current recalcitrance.

Ongoing Benefits (Strategy A)

Turning to the related section of table 4-2, we see that employed women who want changes from their husbands in the highly salient and significant autonomy and chore areas argue that their husbands owe concessions to them because of all wives have already done and are doing for them. They believe that husbands are now morally obligated to reciprocate in ways that are exceedingly important to these working women.

For example, the variable called "wife-impact on social class position" rests on the notion that women who earn more money (and are better-educated and more sex-role modern) are more likely to believe that their own efforts have contributed to their husbands' economic well-being (compare table 3-2). Therefore, because wives supply more dollars, husbands are now morally obligated to grant concessions and make changes. Undoubtedly, dollars are not the sole element supplied and subsumed under "I do so much for him," but apparently money is at least one salient element. These employed wives, by virtue of their income, have increased household social standing in their own eyes and in the eyes of important peers and kin. Consequently, they feel their husbands are now obligated to reciprocate by changing with regard to the dispute at hand.

Among nonemployed wives, strategy A also tends to be utilized in conflicts over chores. Their definition of this type of situation may reflect the *quid pro quo* idea referred to earlier. Such wives may reason that they have made significant inputs into the household over the years in the form of housekeeping chores and that therefore their husbands should take that into account and reciprocate, including a willingness to change and share in these very same chores.

Wives' Interests (F-2)

The response coded F-2 was one supplied by the women themselves (11.3 percent) in replying to the question about bargaining strategies utilized. The argument is based on the premise that the changes wives want their husbands to make are in wives' best interests. Typical comments were: "It would make me happier." "I feel he should because he loves me and therefore should try to make me happy." "Because I want him to, and because it would improve our marriage." "Because it would help our relationship be better." "Just because I want him to." "Because I wanted it." "Because I want it—because I feel it's necessary." "I just think it's my right, and I have to pursue it." "Because it bothers me, and that should be enough." "Because I want this for myself, and he should want it for me too."

Underlying F-2 is a strong strain of what is described throughout this book as women's orientations towards egalitarianism or individualistic rights and privileges. Some women do indeed rely on such strategies in negotiations with their husbands and are not hesitant to volunteer the information. Although this may not be their sole strategy, it is one means that they utilize to seek to get their husbands to change their behaviors. However, as the percentage cited indicates, it is nowhere near the most frequently utilized negotiating point. (Nearly 68 percent of respondents reported using the family-oriented strategy C, as compared to 11.3 percent here.) Very likely strategy F-2 is more prevalent now than one or two decades ago, however, and will probably become increasingly more frequent during the years ahead.

Table 4-3 shows that for employed women, disputes over expressive behaviors lead them to negotiate with their husbands in terms of wives' own interests. They contend that if their husbands changed, they (wives) would be better off. Nonemployed women, however, reveal that conflicts over the autonomy issue stimulate them to utilize this particular bargaining strategy. In both instances, sex-role modernity also exerts positive influence in the expected direction. Workers who revealed greater modernity on the RLM dimension, and nonworkers who are more egalitarian on both IE and SA (compare figure 1-1) explicitly contend with their husbands on the basis of wives' own self-interest.

The strategy E section of table 4-2 showed that workers do not resort to the "husband-duty" strategy to resolve conflicts over expressiveness. Instead, as we now see in table 4-3, they opt for a more explicitly self-interest approach. Their husbands should change their socioemotional behaviors, not primarily because it is their responsibility as husbands to do so, but chiefly because it is best for wives.

Similarly, nonworkers revealed quite emphatically in table 4-2 that they do not resort to a collective strategy ("it's best for the entire family") to resolve disputes over their autonomy. Instead, these wives too prefer to stress individualistic interests ("it's best for me if he changes in this matter").

Clearly, expressiveness and autonomy are exceedingly vital issues. Workers probably feel they have already gotten a relative degree of autonomy and independence by virtue of their labor-force participation. Therefore, what probably ranks next in importance for them, in terms of gratifications that husbands can supply, is the expressive dimension.

Table 4-3
Influences on Choice of Bargaining Strategies F-2, F-1, and B, and on Strategy Used Most Frequently, by Employment Status

Workers			Nonworkers		
Is Strategy F-2 Used?[a]					
	beta	r		beta	r
Conflict-expressive	+.33	.36	Conflict-autonomy	+.22	.22
1971 RLM modernity	+.20	.24	1975 IE modernity	+.19	.19
Husband education	+.16	.22	Marriage-age	−.22	−.16
1971 Children intended	−.10*	−.15	Father's job status	+.18	.17
Catholic	−.10*	−.09	1971 SA modernity	+.15	.19
$MR = .47, R^2 = .22, n = 137$			$MR = .42, R^2 = .18, n = 184$		

Workers			Nonworkers		
Is Strategy F-1 Used?[a]					
	beta	r		beta	r
Conflict-misc.	+.30	.31	Conflict-economic	+.22	.29
1975 TH modernity	+.24	.29	Husband fair	+.21	.23
Impact of husband on future living standard	+.13	.13	1974 Earnings	+.18	.24
Job satisfaction	−.14	−.15	1975 Children intended	−.13	−.14
Husband shares clothes washing	+.12	.24	Premarital job	+.11	.12
Wife impact-social class	−.11*	−.11			
$MR = .49, R^2 = .24, n = 134$			$MR = .43, R^2 = .18, n = 183$		

Workers			Nonworkers		
Is Strategy B Used?[a]					
	beta	r		beta	r
Husband shares clothes washing	+.25	.26	1975 Companionship	−.18	−.21
1974 Husband income	−.11*	−.17	1975 Parity	−.15	−.15
Social class-husband	−.10*	−.15	Aspirations for husband	−.11	−.14
			Wife responsible for childcare	+.11*	.13
$MR = .32, R^2 = .10, n = 136$			$MR = .30, R^2 = .09, n = 184$		

Table 4-3 continued

Workers			Nonworkers		
Type of Strategy Used Most Frequently[b]					
	beta	r		beta	r
1975 TH modernity	+.35	.37	Conflict-autonomy	+.24	.25
Internal resources	+.23	.27	Conflict-		
1971 Birth			expressive	+.23	.24
intentions	−.24	−.19	1975 TM modernity	+.20	.22
Child-difference	+.21	.18	Conflict-children	−.14	−.20
Conflict-children	−.20	−.22			
Husband shares					
cooking	+.15	.17			
Aspirations for					
husband	+.15	.21			
MR = .61, R² = .38, n = 135			MR = .43, R² = .19, n = 182		

All betas significant at .05, unless starred.

[a]Positive score = yes.

[b]Positive score = individualistic strategies.

And just as gender-role modernity acts as a driving force for workers, it does the same among nonworkers. The pattern may be as follows: Over the years, these women have been able to negotiate less autonomy from their husbands than have workers. As a result, conflict over autonomy is a much more painful issue than is expressiveness. Therefore, it follows that the more radically egalitarian (IE) they prefer their spouses to behave, and the more radically innovative they prefer their own behaviors to be (SA), the more strongly do they utilize self-interest techniques to press for actual spouse concessions with regard to their autonomy and independence.

Interestingly enough, nonworkers who married earlier also tend to use strategy F-2. It may be that those who married younger feel most keenly their lack of autonomy. When they married, they probably had few preferences for autonomy. However, over the years, their role traditionalism may have become modified for a variety of reasons. (Compare chapter 1.) Currently, they may desire autonomy as strongly as some better-educated women who married later and in past years may have actually experienced considerable autonomy.

In hindsight, it is clear that the statement "because it is best for me" should have been read to *all* respondents when they were asked about their bargaining strategies. Had that been done, it is certain that many more women would have reported using that strategy than those who actually volunteered it. Future investigations cannot overlook it, because it is fraught with such significance in terms of the conflict issues with which it is associated, and also because of its connections with gender-role modernity and marital changes.

The emergence of a self-interest bargaining strategy is serendipitous. At the time of data collection, the idea of asking women whether they negotiated with their husbands on the grounds that changes in the husbands' behavior would be better for wives was thought to be inappropriate. Allegedly, wives did not negotiate that way; or if they did, it was assumed, they would be hesitant to admit it. Because of the romantic-love complex and what that implies in terms of altruism, self-giving, and so forth, it was thought that self-interest strategies would conjure up in the mind of the respondent what Homans (1974) calls "horrid profit-seeking." It seemed that "people in love" simply did not negotiate that way. However, it turns out that some women do; and they also negotiate in terms of strategies which, while not explicitly labled as self-interest, are allied to it, namely, strategies A, B, D, and F-1.

Husbands' Interests (F-1)

As we have just seen, when respondents were asked to supply any other bargaining strategies, over 11 percent mentioned arguments based on wives' best interests. But 8.5 percent indicated that they argued it is in their husbands' best interests to change. It is essentially better for him to stop or start doing something in relation to the conflict issue in question. One respondent actually used the phrase, "It's for his own best interest." Others said, "Because it's best for him," or "Because it could be pleasurable for him," or "Because it would help him to eventually have a better image of himself." It is therefore instructive to look at the use of this strategy by both workers and nonworkers respectively.

Employed Women and the Use of Strategy F-1. Giving attention to the variables with the two strongest betas in the corresponding section of table 4-3, we find, first, that workers who dispute with husbands over what were called "miscellaneous annoyances and complaints" tend to rely on this particular method of bargaining to try to resolve those kinds of conflicts. The annoyances seemed to consist of desires on the part of wives to improve certain characteristics in their husbands. Wives wanted husbands to "shape up," and to stop being passive, stop mumbling, become patient, become gregarious, become physically fit, become religious, and so forth. Since those were the issues, it seems eminently plausible that wives' negotiating strategies would be couched in terms of husbands' own best interests, which indeed turns out to be the case.

Nonetheless, that does not mean that wives fail to perceive that their own welfare would also be enhanced if husbands altered their behaviors in the prescribed fashion. Therefore, while the apparent motive for change is Other's well-being, an important secondary motive is Actor's own immediate well-being.

That possibility suggests that the distinction between Actor's and Other's interests may not always be clear. Some writers such as Ekeh (1974) draw a sharp cleavage. Others tend to argue for their intermixture and overlap (Ellis, 1971); fulfillment of one set of interests may sometimes contribute to the other set as well.

The second strongest influence on opting for strategy F-1 among employed women is rejection of traditional preferences regarding husband role behaviors. The greater the sex-role modernity, the more likely workers are to raise these particular annoyance issues and to press their husbands to change by arguing that it is in the husbands' best interests to do so. Conversely, holding to what has been described as the "anachronistic" (Scanzoni, 1975b) preferences that make up TH apparently leads women to hold their husbands more in "awe and reverence." These women may be less likely to perceive faults, flaws, and annoyances in their husbands and/or be less likely to dispute openly about them and/or to negotiate on these bases.

What the long-term consequences of this particular effect of gender modernity might be would require subsequent interviews to determine. It could be argued that, should conflict of this sort be resolved by husbands actually making the desired changes, there would be greater feelings of maximum joint profit (MJP) and increased system solidarity. Nonetheless, husbands may come to resent strongly their egalitarian wives continually pressing them on these kinds of issues (which husbands might consider petty), thus resulting in reduced solidarity and increased likelihood of dissolution.

Nonemployed Women and the Use of Strategy F-1. Moving to the pertinent section of table 4-3, we observe that for nonworkers, a different issue—economics—predicts use of strategy F-1. Wives who want their husbands to stop spending "too much" money, or to start spending more, argue that it is in their husbands' own best interests to change behaviors. Nevertheless, they recognize the fairness of their husbands' counterposition, as indicated by the emergence of that variable in the data.

The matter of wives also profiting by changes on the part of their husbands may be an even more important consideration for nonworkers than for workers, since here the issue under dispute is the economic dimension. The finding that nonworkers report this issue on connection with F-1 may be the result of not having any income of their own to control directly. For instance, if the husbands of employed women err in their consumption behaviors, those women can compensate because of their own independent resources, whereas nonemployed women cannot. Nevertheless, simultaneous with their disagreement, is the realization by nonworkers that their spouses do after all earn virtually all the family income. That fact, therefore, prompts them to ascribe (although grudgingly, perhaps) a certain degree of equity to their husbands' judgments on how to spend their own earnings.

At the same time, nonworkers who had some 1974 income perceive that that fact puts them in a relatively better bargaining position. They can point to the potential of their reentering the labor force and thus gaining income once again should their spouses refuse to change. Hence, their potential alternative resources influence them to press for economic change on their husbands' part and also to argue that it is best for husbands to do so.

But implicit in such a bargaining stance is the fact that such a change would enhance wives' interests as well. In short, there often is no absolute distinction between individual and dyadic interests. Whether or not what is profitable for the dyad is also beneficial for the individual becomes an empirical question, as does the reverse—the conditions under which individual profit does or does not contribute to dyadic well-being.

Promised Inducements (Strategy B)

The matter of reciprocity appears once again in a different form in the bargaining strategy utlized by the smallest proportion of respondents (6.8 percent), namely, strategy B: "He should because then I'll do something he wants."

Heath (1976) draws a distinction between the usual sociological approach to reciprocity as enunciated, for example, by Gouldner (1960) and that generally enunciated by economists. Sociologists tend to emphasize that Other is currently obligated to Actor because of the benefits that Actor supplied to Other in time past and continues to supply (that is essentially captured in strategy A, as discussed earlier). Among economists, on the other hand, according to Heath, strategy B is common. It is what Ekeh (1974) calls an inducement-type strategy. Heath suggests that underlying this form of negotiation is faith or trust in the opposing actor or group; it is basically a future orientation.

Wives use this strategy by telling their husbands that they should change their behavior because if they do, then wives will respond with a particularly beneficial input. "You do something for me, and I'll do something for you." In contrast stands strategy A: "I have *already* done something for you, now you are morally obligated to do something for me." An illustration of strategy A occurred during December, 1976, when the Saudi Arabian government kept oil price increases to a minimum as compared with other oil-producing nations. Their government announced that since they had done the United States a favor, they now expected an American gesture of gratitude and rectitude with respect to the Middle East political situation. In contrast, strategy B is illustrated in the stance of other oil-producing nations which say to America, "If you achieve a peace settlement, then we will guarantee you oil."

Use of that sort of bargaining strategy (B) by workers is explained most strongly by one of the household-chore variables discussed in table 3-3.

Employed women, in households where wives report that clothes washing is already more of a shared duty, tend to employ strategy B. Thus, for some wives, the process of being successful in negotiating their husbands to participate in this chore has ignited a pattern of seeking to resolve conflicts through future-oriented bargains. It may be that in order to negotiate husbands into doing that chore, wives had to promise some future benefit in return. Presumably, because that bargaining strategy worked, these wives then tend to draw on it again to resolve other regulated conflicts.

Group Versus Individualistic Strategies

When Actor presents reasons to Other to get Other to change, Actor is in effect engaging in bargaining to try to overcome Other's resistance to change. Among respondents reporting regulated disputes, only 4 percent reported that they gave no reasons to achieve change. Hence, most women do respond to husband resistance with "struggle"—at least in the form of attempts to negotiate some sort of resolution. We have seen that in their efforts to persuade their husbands to change, wives tend to use either group-oriented or individualistic arguments. Now the question becomes: Is it possible to identify more precisely the conditions under which wives opt for group-oriented as opposed to individualistic approaches?

After respondents were asked to name the reasons they gave their husbands in their efforts to convince their husbands they should change, respondents were then asked, "Which is the reason you use most often?" Among those respondents who reported using some strategy, the percentages reporting using each category most are given in figure 4-2.

That figure is a continuum reflecting collective to individualistic bargaining strategies. At the polar collectivist (or group) end are cases who responded with C. At the polar individualistic end are cases who responded with F-2. Just below F-2 are cases responding with F-1, based on the above discussion that concern for husbands' well-being closely parallels wives' individualistic interests. Below F-1 come strategies B, A, D, and E, respectively. Based on the logic of the preceding section of this chapter, what has been devised is an index of increasingly collective or group-oriented negotiating strategies. Certainly E belongs above C at the collective pole. Strategy B appears to be more individualistic than A, and A more so than D. Strategy D is placed toward the center of the continuum because it presumably contains both collective and individualistic elements.

Figure 4-2 also portrays the construction of the variable explained in the last section of table 4-3. That variable measures the type of negotiating strategy used most frequently on a continuum from collective (low score) to individualistic (high score).[11]

Individualistic

- - - - Strategy F-2 (8%): Wife's own best interests.

- - - - Strategy F-1 (7%): Husband's best interests.

- - - - Strategy B (3%): "He should because then I'll do something he wants."

- - - - Strategy A (4%): "He should because I do so much for him."

- - - - Strategy D (22%): "Because it's only right and fair."

- - - - Strategy E (11%): Husband's responsibility or duty.

- - - - Strategy C (45%): Best interests of the entire family.

Collectivist

Figure 4-2. Continuum of Bargaining Strategies Used Most Frequently

Employed Women and Strategies Used Most Frequently

Among workers, the strongest predictor is gender-role modernity: women who are more TH egalitarian opt for the more individualistic bargaining strategies. Conversely, those who are more traditional in terms of the husbands' ascribed position tend to opt more for group-oriented bargaining strategies.

Therefore, as was theoretically predictable, gender role does influence the frequency of strategies actually utilized to try to overcome regulated conflict. Gender-role preferences are, as Holter (1970) argues, a way of structuring preferred rewards and acceptable costs—a means of establishing priorities or desired profit. The more strongly workers seek for modern goals, the more they tend to opt for negotiating strategies that reflect those kinds of interests. Conversely, women who seek traditional interests, that is, interests that prescribe that a woman's major life gratifications come via husband and children—those women negotiate precisely on those very bases.

Recall from chapter 1 that 1971 gender-role modernity predicted fewer births intended and that, by 1975, women who in 1971 had intended to have fewer children actually had fewer. Simultaneously, those women who intended to have fewer children now (in 1975) negotiate less in terms of group-strategies and more in terms of self-interest approaches (table 4-3). For example, fewer children make it simpler for workers to negotiate husbands into childcare arrangements that enhance women's occupational pursuits. Thus, gender modernity maintains a long-term influence on bargaining via its effects on fertility control. In my earlier investigation (1975b), the consequences of fertility control for bargaining were not foreseen—only that effective fertility control would in general enhance women's self-interest. The specific finding in table 4-3 adds a concrete dimension to the understanding of how that comes about.

A second fertility variable in the equation is the difference in unplanned pregnancies between 1971 and 1975. The greater this difference (or the more unintended pregnancies that occurred between 1971 and 1975), the more the women opt for self-interest strategies. There appears to be no connection between this fertility variable and 1971 birth intentions, due to their miniscule correlation (.03). Evidently, an unforeseen pregnancy has its own peculiar consequences. Working women may perceive such pregnancies (and births) as especially costly to their own occupational interests. Thus, since some children are ill-timed, these wives define their own interests as being especially undermined; therefore, to overcome that situation, they bargain with those interests uppermost.

Interestingly enough, the particular conflict that appears is child-discipline. Wives who report this issue opt more for group rather than individualistic strategies. As was noted in connection with strategy C, when the conflict is over the interests of children and thus the total family group, the arguments used to resolve the dispute are less likely to be individualistic.

Another significant variable is the internal-resources measure described in figure 2-2. Two of the four items in that index deal explicitly with negotiations with husbands and a third is closely allied to such processes. It turns out that women who perceive that they possess higher levels of those resources tend to opt for self-interest strategies. Chapter 2 indicated that internal resources were influenced by external resources, which in turn were affected by sex-role modernity. Women who do not possess these internal resources opt for traditional ways to try to resolve conflict—ways deemed best for the family as a whole. In other words, they choose strategies along the collective end of the continuum. Conversely, the possession of these internal resources by gender-modern women leads such women to try to resolve conflicts in ways that are specifically beneficial to themselves. Their strategies are chosen from the individualistic end of the continuum.

A remaining predictor of individualistic strategies among these employed women is whether husbands share cooking duties (table 3-3). That behavior is influenced by, among other factors, wives' external resources. Women who possess more of those resources have already negotiated husbands into sharing a household chore. That sharing is in the best interests of those wives. In turn, that successful negotiating process influences workers to continue to press their husbands on grounds of their own interests.

Nonemployed Women and Strategies
Used Most Frequently

Among nonworkers (table 4-3), three conflict issues—along with gender-role preferences—have predictable influences. Disputes over autonomy and socioemotional behaviors lead these wives to opt most frequently for individualistic bargaining approaches. Gender-role modernity (TM) has the same self-interest effect for nonemployed women as it does for employed women. Child-conflicts, on the other hand, tend to result in group strategies. Therefore, whether women currently work or not, the basic syndrome used to try to resolve conflicts is nonetheless similar. In both cases, the particular issues in dispute and the degree of sex-role modernity exercise theoretically predictable influences on whether wives opt more for negotiations based on collective well-being or on individualistic well-being.

Summary and Conclusions

In this chapter, we have traced the steps outlined in figure 4-1. The overarching question has been: What changes are taking place in the ways that women contest their husbands? As women press for the greater symmetry and egalitarianism discussed in prior chapters is there evidence that gender-role preferences are related to conflict behavior that will aid them in achieving those goals?

The answer is that sex roles appear to be as significantly pervasive in accounting for key conflict processes as they were in accounting for the patterns reported in earlier chapters. Nonworkers, for instance, who are more gender-modern are more likely to report the presence of conflict that husbands regulate (and over which men have more power) than women who are more traditional.

However, the major impact of gender roles is on the kinds of negotiating strategies used by women (whether they are employed or not) to try to replace the conflict with a fair exchange. What often stimulates a particular strategy is the nature of the dispute itself. For instance, if the conflict directly affects the entire household (a collective issue), then group-oriented negotiating strategies are used. And it turns out that sex-role-traditional wives who have more children are more likely to negotiate in terms of the good of the household as a whole.

Conversely, when the dispute is over something that more directly affects the woman herself (for example, autonomy or expressiveness), she resorts to individualistic bargaining strategies. Sex-role-modern wives (with fewer children) who possess high levels of intangible resources tend to bargain on the basis of individualistic interests. The traditional woman negotiates with the goal in view of group well-being, group solidarity. Her own interests are submerged into those of the group. If the family does well, she does too; and that satisfies her.

The modern woman, on the other hand, is less likely to submerge her own interests or goals to those of the group. She is concerned about gaining her own interests, as well as seeing that her husband and children gain theirs also. Her guiding philosophy is—if I do well, the family does too. But simultaneously, the family does well if other parts (not just she) do well too (Gerson, 1976). In order to maintain that delicate balance, she tries not to allow her interests to become subordinated to those of her husband. She refuses to have her interests abnegated. Instead, her goal is to negotiate outcomes that are fair to all parties concerned, including herself. This concern for the justice of her own individualistic interests, which marks the modern woman, is missing from the negotiating behaviors of role-traditional wives.

As was true for the patterns of earlier chapters, these contrasts in negotiating processes are probably more common today than they were two or more decades ago. Moreover, the modern bargaining style is likely to become even more common in the years ahead.

Bartos (1974) defines the tough bargainer as one who makes high demands and grants few concessions. As more women become increasingly more gender egalitarian, they are likely to become increasingly tougher bargainers. That is, they will become ever more unreceptive to the traditional idea that family happiness is the result of appeasing the resident male. Instead, to use Strauss's (1978) terminology, we may expect them to be continually "testing and stretching the negotiating limits" so that eventually in contrast to the present, there may be no marital issue that is not negotiable. Part of the impetus for this long-term development is likely to be the emerging notion that collective well-being means that a woman's individualistic goals must be regarded and met as seriously as those of her husband and children.

Notes

1. As explained in note 12 of chapter 2, only those variables with significant correlations are used in the equations. That pattern has been followed in chapters 2 and 3 and will be followed in chapters 4 and 5. An additional point needs to be made regarding discussion of all the variables that appear in each equation in all four chapters. I do not discuss all of them for reasons of parsimony. Generally only those variables with the strongest betas are considered. To do otherwise would unnecessarily protract the length of the chapter and, in most instances, would not add a great deal to our understanding of the particular issue in question. Those independent variables that make the most difference in the dependent variables are considered carefully, and they are woven into the overarching theoretical framework that subsumes all the materials in all chapters.

2. The variable called "empathy" has been used and explained in several places (Scanzoni, 1970, 1975a, 1975b). It is defined as "the intellectual

identification with or vicarious experiencing of the feelings, thoughts, or attitudes of another . . . " (Scanzoni, 1970). It is based on an index composed of the following items: *Communication:* "How do you feel about the ways you and your husband can confide in each other, talk things over, and discuss anything that comes up? Do you feel it is very good, O.K., or not so good?" *Understanding:* "How do you feel about the way your husband understands your problems and feelings? Do you feel his understanding is very good, OK, or not so good?"

3. Recall that in connection with figure 2-1 the interviewer said to R: "I am going to read some different kinds of abilities . . . " One that is not listed in figure 2-1 (because factor analyses showed that it did not "load" or belong to the remaining three factors displayed there) is this item: "Managing the Family Budget." This is the single item that appears in panel 1, and in certain following panels.

4. These economic satisfactions are described in note 19, chapter 2.

5. "Companionship" (see Scanzoni, 1970) is measured using the following item: "How do you feel about the companionship that you and your husband have in doing things together during leisure or nonwork time—things such as movies, picnics, and so on. Do you feel the companionship is very good, OK, or not so good?"

6. Coital frequency was measured using the following item borrowed from Ryder and Westoff (1971): "In the past four weeks, approximately how many times have you had intercourse?"

7. See chapter 1 for a discussion of why, in the literature, "bargaining" and "negotiation" tend to be used interchangeably.

8. $n = 353$. Fifteen of the 368 cases reported no strategy. The n of 368 represents women living with husbands in 1975 *and* who report a regulated conflict.

9. Parity explains 8 percent of the variance, more than any other single variable.

10. r of poor or lower empathy with greater numbers of children = $-.38$.

11. The six codes that make up the variable range from *zero* (strategy C) through *five* (strategy F-2).

Bargaining Power and Its Consequences

Earlier in this book, power was defined as the capability to achieve intended goals despite resistance. Given the critiques of marital power in Cromwell and Olson (1975) and Scanzoni (1978), it is unnecessary to examine that literature in detail. Unfortunately, many investigators (Sprey excepted) measured power in isolation from intrinsically related processes such as negotiation, conflict, and change. It was somehow assumed that power could be isolated from adjoining social processes such as those depicted in figure 5-1.

For instance, we have already seen that husbands' power is inseparable from the notion that the husbands are regulating a dispute that wives cannot end. In such a dispute, therefore, the balance of power is tipped in the husband's favor. Wives' definitions of how fair the husband is in his control of the dispute enabled us to assess whether or not his power is legitimate.

Wives' Bargaining Power

It is now time to go beyond the earlier conclusion that wives have relatively less power than husbands over the disputes in question. What needs to be done is to determine what might account for variations in a couple's balance of power. Wives have just reported the bases on which they bargain with spouses to get them to change, or "make him see things your way." The next question has to do with what happens as a result of the negotiations: "Do you succeed? Do you get him to change?"

By asking and answering these kinds of questions, the focus becomes the amount of power wives perceive they have. Power is "the capability to achieve intended effects (or goals) during bargaining and negotiations" (Scanzoni, 1978:549). "Power as process is inseparable from negotiations as process. . . . The exercise of power in these negotiations can produce changes. . . . or it can maintain the status quo. . . . To insert 'power' at this point . . . speaks to Sprey's notion (1975) of power as an 'intervening' factor. It cannot be fully analyzed or explained apart from its antecedents, its consequences, its correlates" (Scanzoni, 1978:549).

In the "real world," conflict, negotiation, and power are as intertwined as bonded chemical elements. Analytically, the chemist abstracts elements from each other and from the whole of which they are a part. Similarly, conflict, legitimacy of husband-power, and wife negotiation were abstracted and opera-

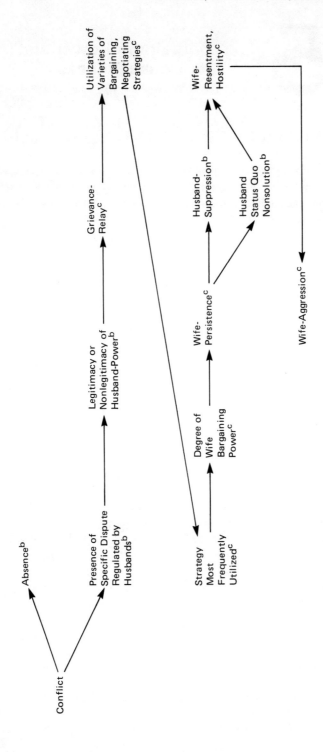

[a]Compare figure 4-1.
[b]As perceived by wives.
[c]Wives' reported behavior.

Figure 5-1. More Complete Ongoing Progression of Processes in which Husbands Are Attempting to Maintain Regulation of Conflict and Wives Are Attempting to Replace That with a Fair Exchange[a]

tionalized separately. (Compare figure 4-1.) The same procedure is followed for wife-power and the remaining elements in figure 5-1. However, one must never lose sight of the premise that in reality they are an intrinsic whole.

The goal was to approximate Sprey's ideal, as nearly as possible, to get family members "to tell us what happens in terms of moves and countermoves, threats and promises, aggression, and appeasement" (1972:237). Based on that goal, once respondents reported their negotiating strategy (as discussed in the preceding chapter), they were asked: "When you tell him your opinion about this matter, does he:

1. Explain why he doesn't do what you want,
2. Compromise and change,
3. Listen but do nothing,
4. Refuse to even listen to you?"

Recall that the respondent has just described how she bargains to bring about change. If she then responds with item 2, she would in effect achieve change. She would have accomplished her intended goal, and that by definition is power. In Heath's (1976) terms, she would be exercising "bargaining power," emphasizing how inseparable power is from adjoining processes.

Within the four-point continuum represented by the four responses, item 2 represents maximum wife-power. The woman might not get all she wanted in terms of the particular conflict issue, but she gets enough of a compromise on her husband's part to warrant calling that change (Bartos, 1974). And she has brought it about through the negotiations analyzed in chapter 4. Those negotiations have enabled her to get at least part of what she wants; she has exercised some power. However, only 21.1 percent of wives responded with item 2.

Furthermore, from additional probing, it became apparent that often husbands will change for a period of time and then revert back to their prior behavior. The situation seems to be much like nations negotiating treaties to regulate offshore fishing rights. For a time, the agreements are observed; but subsequently the vessels of one or the other nations begin gradually to fish where they previously agreed not to fish, to catch species they previously agreed to spare, and so forth.

Analogously, husbands appear to change, revert back, and then go on fluctuating. In effect, that appears to be the essence of institutionalized—or ongoing—conflict. What is being monitored is what Sprey (1972:237) calls "moves and countermoves . . . promises."

In any event, while some wives report they can get their husbands to change (item 2) at least for a while, 31 percent responded with item 1. These women had sufficient power to at least get their husbands to explain why they are behaving as they are and why they insist on regulating the conflict issue as they do. In other words, these wives reported that they are able to persuade their husbands to defend their position and their power. In reality, of course, the type of male response represented by item 1 tends to shift our focus back toward the bargaining process. (The same shift is true for item 2, for it is only out of the negotiations that compromise and change could possibly emerge.)

As long as the negotiations continue, compromise and change remain live and viable options. The wife currently lacks maximum power to effect change, but she has sufficient power to keep the negotiations going. The husband, by maintaining the status quo, is exercising more power than she—though she has enough power to keep him willing to talk. Therefore, eventual change cannot be ruled out. Congressional committees, for example, have enough power to bring witnesses to explain why they continue doing something that some members of Congress wish they would stop doing. The witnesses are supposed to keep on talking to the committees; but in the absence of new legislation, Congress most often lacks sufficient power actually to change the behavior of the witnesses and the interest groups they represent. Item 1 represents an analogous situation.

The single most frequent response (43 percent) was item 3. The wife in this case is saying that when she tries to negotiate, the husband listens but makes no meaningful response of any sort. Of the three categories described so far, this one obviously characterizes least wife-power. The only part of her goals or objectives that she is able to accomplish is getting him to listen. Beyond that, she has no power over her husband—she has no capabilities to move toward her goal of replacing the conflict with a fair exchange.

Finally, item 4 represents the least frequent response (5 percent). Only a small number of wives are willing to acknowledge that their power is virtually nil. They cannot even get their husbands to listen to any of their bargaining strategies. Obviously, therefore, they have no chance at all to effect change and establish a fair exchange. Lacking any such chances is to say they have no power at all to settle the dispute. They are powerless—or at best, have only the barest minimum of power regarding this particular conflict issue.

Explaining Differences in Wives' Bargaining Power

Assuming, therefore, a continuum from higher to lower wife-power (items 2, 1, 3, and 4 above, respectively), a variable is constructed based on that continuum. Table 5-1 shows several elements that explain differences in wife bargaining power.

Employed Wives and Bargaining Power. Among workers, 1975 empathy satisfactions predict greater power, that is, increased capability to move husbands in the direction either of changing or at least getting them to defend their position. Thus, empathy increases wives' power.

However, satisfactory empathy is positively related to husbands' education.[1] Validation of the notion that wives of higher-status husbands are able to wield more power over the dispute comes from one other variable in the panel: The more positively that wives perceive that peers evaluate the living standard provided them (wives) by their husbands, the more power wives report for themselves. In short, higher status husbands appear to be more amenable to wives' bargaining power, a point that was implied early in the preceding chapter.

Furthermore, note that the data reveal that if wives judge husbands to be fair in the exercise of husbands' power, the more power wives claim for themselves. This may be compared to the finding reported in table 4-1, which showed that fairness is predicted by empathy. Therefore, empathy has both an important indirect as well as direct impact on employed wives' power.

It is particularly intriguing to consider the positive association between wife-power and legitimate husband-power. Apparently, unfair husband-power tends to be more inflexible and rigid. To be unfair is to be unwilling to concede very much during bargaining. It may sometimes include unwillingness to bargain (or discuss) at all.

On the other hand, fairness is probably associated with greater flexibility and willingness to make certain concessions and accommodations to wives. Thus, in a very real sense, the definition of fairness that wives ascribe to husbands is intimately tied to negotiation. Earlier, it was indicated that fairness tends to be linked to resources supplied in exchange for demands made. Apparently, it is while spouses bargain that such deals are made. In this instance, the husband holds a goal that the wife wants to change or at least modify. To the degree that (higher-status) husbands combine greater resources with certain concessions, wives are more likely to think their husbands' power in this particular interest sphere is legitimate. Not only have these wives obtained more gratifications in exchange for their conformity; they have also simultaneously been able to reshape that conformity to bring it, if ever so slightly, more into line with their own interests.

In effect, legitimate male power means less male power or control, as compared with their attempts to dominate totally or exercise nonlegitimate power. And less male power means more female power. Therefore, when wives state that their husbands are being fair in their negotiations, they are in essence saying that male power is being limited so that wives can have that much more control.

There is some discrepancy between studies that report wives' power to be positively related to husbands' status and those that report it to be inverse (Scanzoni, 1978). But few studies have attempted to analyze power in a context of ongoing negotiations and empathy. When that sort of complexity is introduced, facile generalizations become pallid indeed. For example, in this particular dispute, husbands retain greater power than wives basically because the husbands are more able to maintain the status quo than wives are able to

Table 5-1
Influences on Wife Bargaining Power and Persistence, and on Attempted Husband Counter Strategies, by Employment Status

Workers			Nonworkers		
Wife Bargaining Power[a]					
	beta	r		beta	r
Husband shares cooking	+.23	.25	1975 Empathy	+.26	.35
Husband-fair	+.16	.24	Husband-fair	+.26	.34
1975 TW modernity	+.16	.18	1971 IE modernity	−.15	−.17
Living standard by peers	+.17	.19	Appreciation resource	+.14	.16
Age last child, 1975	−.18	−.16	Wife-relay	+.11	.17
1975 Empathy	+.14	.20			

$MR = .46, R^2 = .22, n = 134$　　　　　　　　$MR = .49, R^2 = .24, n = 183$

Workers			Nonworkers		
Wife-Persistence[a]					
	beta	r		beta	r
1975 IE modernity	+.19	.26	Strategy D	+.17	.18
1971 Companionship	−.17	−.24	1975 TH modernity	+.11*	.13
Strategy B	+.18	.18			
Wife living standard by peers	+.22	.24			
Wife-power	−.18	−.20			
Wife-relay	+.15	.14			

$MR = .48, R^2 = .23, n = 137$　　　　　　　　$MR = .21, R^2 = .05, n = 184$

Workers			Nonworkers		
Attempted Husband-Suppression[a]					
	beta	r		beta	r
Wife-power	−.25	−.28	1975 Empathy	−.17	.25
Conflict-autonomy	+.26	.25	Appreciation resource	+.14	.23
Husband shares food-shopping	−.16	−.18	1975 IE modernity	+.22	.23
1975 Economic satisfaction	−.12	−.18	1975 Children intended	−.10*	−.21
Wife-relay	−.11*	−.15	Strategy B	+.15	.20
			1975 Children unwanted	+.14	.24
			External resource	+.13	.21

$MR = .45, R^2 = .20, n = 141$　　　　　　　　$MR = .49, R^2 = .24, n = 184$

Table 5-1 continued

Workers			Nonworkers		
Attempted Husband Status Quo Solution[a]					
	beta	r		beta	r
Father's job			Budget-resource	−.22	−.20
status	−.24	−.30	1975 Economic		
Job status	−.20	−.28	satisfaction	−.18	−.16
Husband respon-			Strategy B	+.13	.17
sible-repairs	−.21	−.16	Conflict-		
1975 TM modernity	−.15	−.27	economic	+.12	.13
Continuity	−.13	−.22			
$MR = .48, R^2 = .23, n = 136$			$MR = .33, R^2 = .11, n = 184$		

All betas significant at .05, except where starred.

[a]Higher score = greater power, or persistence, or attempted suppression, or else status quo solution.

change it. But the relative degree of wife-power (as measured by wives' success in negotiations, including keeping them going) is increased if women have higher-status husbands with whom they experience greater empathy. Presumably, therefore, because males have, say, greater economic resources than women (compare chapter 3), they have greater power to regulate the dispute more in their favor. But simultaneously, wives of higher-status husbands share more power with their husbands (than do other wives) because of the greater empathy experienced and its impact on bargaining processes.

Thus far, the discussion has centered mostly around variation in wives' power depending on husbands' resources. But power variation also depends on preferences and resources that these employed women bring to the negotiations. The "wife bargaining power" section of table 5-1, for instance, shows that modern sex-role preferences predict greater wife-power. Just as modernity influenced individualistic bargaining strategies, modernity has a significant impact on power itself. Workers who are less role-traditional apparently tend to press their husbands more and are able to bring about greater changes in their behaviors.

This is a theoretically predictable finding—and one that is highly important in terms of identifying any long-term changes in marriage patterns. If women are becoming more gender-role egalitarian, then they are more likely to press for more equitable power balances in marriage in order to be better able to pursue their own interests both inside and outside of marriage.

At the same time, the data reveal another key element that workers utilize to try to increase their current bargaining power. The more these wives have already gotten their husbands to share the chore of cooking, the more power the wives now have in this current dispute. Recall from table 3-3 that shared cooking is predicted by greater wife-to-husband 1974 income ratio, external resources, and SA modernity. The closer a wife's own tangible resources approximated those of her husband, the more she was able to exercise bargaining power to get him to share several chores, including cooking.

Those resources now operate on the struggles of these women to resolve this conflict. Having been successful in past bargaining, they are relatively more successful in current bargaining. Simultaneously, intangible resources also operate on the earlier chore questions and thus operate indirectly on current disputes. Likewise, gender-role modernity operates indirectly on current power struggles by influencing wives' incomes, past chore arrangements, and external resources. Thus, a whole range of elements appears to have enhanced these employed wives' power in earlier negotiations and perhaps actual disputes. Once a pattern of having had power is established by workers, they seem better able to continue to exercise it in the present.

Therefore, the pattern that emerges out of these several threads is that while husbands effectively control the current dispute, some wives are able to make inroads on that power because of their increased mutual empathy. Furthermore, wives made additional inroads when they had greater tangible and intangible resources that enabled them to strike more favorable bargains in the past. Added to this syndrome are the indirect and direct influences of sex-role modernity.

Nonemployed Wives and Bargaining Power. In table 5-1 we find that among nonworkers, positive empathy has a much stronger effect on wife-power than it did for workers, though for presumably similar reasons. Moreover, being able to relay grievances enhances wife-power, as does husband-fairness.

In contrast to workers, the data give no indication of any tangible resources of nonworkers or any past favorable bargains that nonworkers might utilize as a precedent in current negotiations to achieve their desired ends. The only intangible resource they seem to possess that positively affects their power is indicated by a higher score on their appreciation-type resources.

The absence of any tangible resources may contribute to a significant discrepancy between workers and nonworkers. Among nonworkers, gender-role modernity predicts less wife-power. Note that the sex-role dimension appearing in this section of the table is the "radical" IE dimension. (Compare figure 1-1.) The more strongly that nonworkers prefer innovative husband behaviors, the less power they perceive themselves to hold. In effect, to be more egalitarian is to hold stronger aspirations for change. But nonworkers lack tangible resources with which to actually exercise significant bargaining power.

Therefore, it appears that gender-role-modern nonworkers sense their lack of power more keenly than do gender-role-traditional nonworkers. As Walster and Walster make clear (1975:38), an appeal to the dominant group to change apart from resources with which to bargain is not likely to succeed. For men to accept the behavioral consequences of modern gender preferences, women have to be able to apply appropriate sanctions.

I just made the point that employed wives' power in these conflict issues varies with the degree of legitimate power their husbands exercise. The same pattern holds true for nonemployed women, but with some critical elaboration. Their power is probably much more fully dependent on the power levels chosen by husbands than is true for employed women. Lacking resources of their own to counter husbands' bargaining demands, there is less that nonworkers can do to curb excesses of male power and domination. Consequently, there may be more of a tendency for some nonworkers' husbands to act unfairly and to exercise greater degrees of nonlegitimate power. Nonworkers—particularly those who are more modern in their gender-role preferences—keenly perceive that injustice; consequently, they perceive that their own power has been correspondingly diminished.

An analogy to the notion of *noblesse oblige* is not unwarranted, that is, "the moral obligation of the rich or highborn to display honorable or charitable conduct" (Stein, 1966:969). The issue is—What would motivate nonworkers' husbands to act fairly, given the absence of effective resources on the part of the wife to help bring that about? It turns out that better-educated husbands who provide higher empathy to wives are also more likely to act fairly (table 4-1). Presumably, they do that (in part, at least) out of a sense of moral obligation that their superior position as males compels them to do so. But among less-educated men who provide less empathy, any sense of *noblesse oblige* is more irrelevant; and there is therefore much greater likelihood of domination and exploitation.

Wives' Persistence

In his elaboration of Simmel, Coser (1956) notes that conflicts can either be executed openly by the aggrieved party, or else they can be suppressed. Blau (1964) discusses the same point. Both investigators describe the rationale that often accompanies suppression of conflict: namely, conflict is thought to threaten group harmony, peace, and solidarity. Therefore, it is assumed to be in the group's interest to avoid conflict. And conflict is avoided by not openly expressing grievances, by not pressing for changes on the part of opposing actors.

It was learned earlier (table 4-1) that more than 90 percent of these respondents do not suppress conflict with their husbands over the dispute in question. But given the intervening items, it is now possible to probe this matter in greater depth. Already we have seen that respondents were asked to describe their negotiation strategy(ies) and the degree of wives' bargaining power. The next step in the ongoing progression illustrated in figure 5-1 deals with wives' persistence in pressing their ends.

Respondents were asked, "Do you generally keep trying to tell your husband what you think about this matter or keep quiet about it?"[2] While a wife may have responded to the "relay of grievance" item (described in chapter

4) with a simple "yes," indicating that she is able to tell her husband her opinion "about the way he is in this matter," she may fear to bring up the matter to her husband more than once a month or once every four months or even once a year. Technically, she may not be suppressing the dispute, but her persistence in expressing it may be minimal. Therefore, since we are examining bargaining power, it is appropriate to ascertain how persistent women are in their struggle to resolve the dispute.

Employed Women and Persistence

Among employed women, the strongest correlation (and greatest explained variance, 7 percent) emerges from 1975 IE modernity. (Compare figure 1-1.) As might be expected, workers who prefer innovative changes in husbands' role behaviors tend to be more persistent in pressing for specific changes over the dispute in question. They are less willing to be put off or to accept vague, negative, or ambivalent responses in their efforts to bargain with their husbands. Consequently, role-modern workers not only already have more power, they are also more likely to remain continually in pursuit of still more of it.

Interestingly enough, however, power by itself is a negative predictor of persistence. Most wives who have more power apparently sense less need to be continually pressing their claims, since they are probably more satisfied with the degree of goal attainment they already have. Being able to get husbands to change or else to explain or defend their position reduces the motivation for continued persistence. Some wives have gotten some or most of what they wanted—at least temporarily. Conversely, with more limited power comes greater motivation to keep on pressing husbands for change.

Nevertheless, among that subset of employed women who are the most egalitarian on IE, current power levels, though relatively high, are not deemed high enough; hence, these women keep on striving for even greater authority over the dispute in question (Duke, 1976). For instance, it could be that sex-role-modern women are least likely to allow their husbands to renege on their agreements. Recall that wives report that husbands will verbally grant a concession but later ignore it behaviorally, so that actual resolution never firmly comes about. Gender-modern workers may be more willing to try to hold their husbands to their deals and not allow a gradual return to the status quo ante.

Another strong influence on wife-persistence emerges from a variable similar to (and correlated with, $r = .73$) one explained in table 3-1. There the question was whether their working actually enhances family lifestyle. Here the variable is whether the women thought their peers believed their working had that same effect. If they thought their peers did believe that, they respond that they are more persistent in trying to settle the dispute.

Recall that their own income had strong positive influences on their perception that their job enhanced family lifestyle, and their income is similarly correlated with positive perceptions about peers.[3] Thus, wives with higher earnings perceive that peers view positively their efforts to enhance lifestyle, and that perception helps "cause" them to be persistent in power struggles with their spouses. Evidently, their greater objective resources, plus the reinforcement of significant reference groups, provides the necessary impetus to enable them to keep on bargaining to try to break the deadlock and resolve their dispute in a way that they consider favorable. Conversely, lower income wives with less or no such peer reinforcement tend to be less persistent in their negotiating efforts.

There is also a connection between strategy B (table 4-3) and persistence. Workers who resort to a future-oriented bargaining strategy ("If he changes, then I'll do something for him") are more persistent. Very likely in the "real world" there are complex feedback loops operating between strategy B and persistence. Women who favor future-oriented bargaining may be more likely to be continually proposing incentives to try to get husbands to change. But, simultaneously, being more persistent may force them into that kind of strategy. They may perhaps feel that that may not be the ideal way to bargain; but because they must be persistent to get their husbands to change, they may find it is the most effective (or perhaps the only) way to proceed. In short, there may be an inherent affinity between future-oriented bargaining and being more persistent at attempted conflict resolution.

Nonemployed Women and Persistence

Among nonworkers (table 5-1), only two elements account very modestly for persistence. Persistence may be harder to explain among these women because they probably have less than workers. In any case, being sex-role-modern predicts nonworkers' persistence, as does the use of strategy D (table 4-2). Apparently, nonemployed women persist on the basis of its being only right and fair for their husbands to change their behavior. Wives have conformed to husbands' expectations in the past and now consider it equitable to press for reciprocity.

Suppression by Husbands

Like all of these conflict processes, persistence involves behaviors of both partners. The wife does or does not keep on bargaining for change, and the husband reacts in one fashion or another. Wives have already reported some of those reactions: his fairness and his degree of change. In addition, wives were probed about other reactions of their husbands with this question: "Does he in any way ever try to keep you from bringing up the subject and talking about how you feel about this matter?"[4]

This specific husband regulation strategy might be called suppression or coercive suppression (figure 5-1). The dominant group follows its own best interests by seeking to suppress unrest, keeping the subordinate group quiet, and avoiding confrontation. The theoretical question is the same whether the empirical situation is a government dealing with dissidents or husbands dealing with wives. Suppression of the subordinate group's interests is clearly a way to maintain the dominant group's interests, and indeed to mask the fact that there is any dispute or desire for change at all.

Employed Women and Suppression by Husbands

Table 5-1 displays those variables that account for workers' definitions that their husbands try to engage in suppression. Note that a strong determinant is the balance of power over the dispute. When wives have greater power, their husbands are less likely to engage in attempted suppression; but when wife-power is less, suppression is more likely.

Earlier, it was indicated that simply being able to keep husbands explaining why they do not change increases the likelihood that husbands may eventually shift their bargaining position, if even subtly or slightly. It therefore follows that the possession of gender-role modernity and the empathy and resources to achieve that much power also enables workers to resist attempts at suppression on the part of their husbands. Husbands may seek to suppress the dispute; but the more bargaining power wives have, the more they are able to maintain the ongoing conflict.

Importantly, the data show that where the dispute is over wife-autonomy, attempted suppression is much more likely. Change over this sphere is apparently defined by husbands as exceedingly costly and may be an example of what Coser (1956) labels as basic conflict—that is, conflict over the fundamental rules of an association. By continuing to negotiate with wives over changes that might emerge out of disputes over autonomy, husbands grant a certain degree of legitimacy to those demands. Therefore, the simplest way not to accord legitimacy to such costly demands—and thus to avoid even thinking about actual behavioral changes—is to try to dismiss all mention of the subject. The intent is to keep or coerce wives "from bringing up that sensitive topic." Conversely, where autonomy is not the issue in dispute, husbands appear less likely to attempt to use so radical a conflict strategy.

Furthermore, those employed wives who are more satisfied with the living standard their husbands supply and have already gotten them to share the food-shopping chore tend not to report attempted suppression. Therefore, just as higher-status wives seem more capable of chipping away at husbands' power, so it seems that they are also better able to resist an extreme form of nonlegitimate power—suppression. Likewise, already having gotten husbands to share a chore provides these women with additional leverage in resisting husbands' attempts to refuse to discuss further changes in other areas.

Nonemployed Women and Suppression by Husbands

Among nonworkers, the single strongest predictor of attempted suppression is gender-role modernity. Similarly, wives who score higher on two dimensions of intangible resources (external and appreciation), and who negotiate in terms of future strategies (bargaining strategy B in table 4-3), perceive greater attempted coercion. It would appear that, because of their greater individualism, certain nonworkers may press their husbands more strongly for change (compare previously discussed sections of table 5-1). Yet, they are unable to effect it because they lack objective resources. But due to their continued pressures, husbands may respond with what more egalitarian women define as greater levels of suppression. The analogy is to that of a relatively powerless subordinate group (gender-modern nonworkers) that holds high expectations for change from those who rule, versus a comparably powerless subordinate group (gender-traditional nonworkers) that holds low expectations for change. Chances are it is the former group rather than the latter that will come to define the dominant group as suppressive.

Husbands and Status Quo Solutions

Another counterstrategy husbands might utilize—rather than bargain in good faith to reach a fair exchange—is what might be termed a status quo solution (figure 5-1). Wives were asked, "Does he ever try to talk you out of how you feel?"[5] Here the issue is not suppression, but neither is it negotiation aimed at any actual change whatsoever on his part. Instead, it is a strategy based on the premise that if somehow the subordinate group can be made to believe that it no longer has any dispute to press nor any desire for change, then the conflict can be considered effectively resolved as far as both parties are concerned. It is an effort to return to the status quo ante, that time before the dispute ever emerged, and thus is a way to avoid any costs on the part of the dominant party.

   In interpreting relationships between this variable and its predictors, the same kind of assumption holds that was made in connection with suppression. The dominant group (men) would want to utilize such a solution as a matter of course, because it reduces their costs and maintains their power in regulating conflict to their advantage. Thus, the question to be explained is: Under what conditions are wives able to resist attempted status quo solutions?

Employed Women and Status Quo Solutions

Table 5-1 reveals that the job status of workers' fathers as well as these women's own current job status are positively related to nonuse of a status quo strategy by their husbands. It was argued earlier that women from higher status homes tend to become more gender-role-modern, attain more education, develop more intangible resources, and get higher-status jobs. Evidently, part of this syndrome includes (as an aspect of growing up in those homes) learning to resist status quo solutions to conflict. Currently, the capability of these women to resist such solutions is reinforced by the greater objective resources and the prestige of their own higher-status occupations.

In that same vein, continuity also reinforces resistance to status quo solutions. The more months wives worked during the 1971-1975 period, the less likely they are to report their husbands try to resort to that type of strategy. Another report (Scanzoni, 1979b) revealed that 1971 gender-role modernity had a strong positive effect on continuity and thus, in 1975, an indirect impact on wives' resistance to the status quo strategy. Simultaneously, the data show that wives' current gender-role modernity maintains a direct influence in helping them resist husbands' attempts to return to the status quo. Egalitarian workers tend to see such "solutions" as actually solving nothing and as quite inimical to their own individualistic interests.

Similarly, bargains struck earlier in which husbands are primarily responsible for repair chores also tend to undercut husbands' tendencies to resort to status quo arguments. Recall that this particular chore was the one in which husbands were most likely to procrastinate, that is, to try to maintain the status quo of leaving the chore undone. Because this category of chores has been a traditionally male duty, it is uniquely prone to attempted status quo solutions. Therefore, it is particularly significant to discover that wives' prior experience in negotiating their husbands into actually doing these duties subsequently results in less likelihood that husbands will attempt nonsolutions with regard to their current dispute.

Nonemployed Women and Status Quo Solutions

Among nonworkers, use of bargaining strategy B is positively related to husbands' attempts at a status quo solution. Here, as in "attempted husband suppression," the paths of influence are very likely mutually reinforcing. That is, nonworkers may use a future-oriented bargaining strategy and yet their husbands refuse to change. This apparently leads these wives to define their husbands as being guilty of suppression or else of nonsolution. Concurrently, husbands' coercion and/or nonsolution may stimulate wives to resort (perhaps out of desperation) to this particular bargaining technique (strategy B) in an attempt to make a deal based on "If you do this for me, then I'll do something for you."

Likewise, nonworkers who rank themselves higher on the resource of budget management find that their husbands tend not to resort to status quo arguments.[6] Wives with this resource utilize it to try to prevent husbands from opting for the status quo, particularly if the conflict issue has to do with economic matters. For example, the table reveals that economic disputes do indeed influence husbands to attempt status quo solutions. Presumably, therefore, wives who possess higher levels of the budget management resource are better able to struggle with their husbands to try to arrive at satisfactory economic arrangements, rather than merely return to the prior unsatisfactory situation.

Resentment by Wives

Injustice—or distributive injustice—is generated when Actor or Group is not receiving the kinds of benefits they feel they should, given the degree of power that Other is seeking to exercise over them. Resentment may be defined as the resultant emotional feeling of anger or hostility on the part of the aggrieved actor or group. In the words of Homans (1974:257), the aggrieved party "will feel some degree of anger and display some aggressive behavior toward the source . . . of the injustice. . . . We should be much less interested in injustice if it did not lead so often to anger and aggression."

Homans then carries his argument one step further by saying that hostility may lead to "aggressive behavior [which] may become . . . an instrumental act by which [the aggrieved party] tries to raise to a higher and more just level the amount of reward he gets" (p. 257). Therefore, if resentment actually has that sort of significant influence on the ultimate outcomes of conflict, it becomes quite important to identify what causes it.

Resentment on the Part of Employed Wives

Given Homans' discussion of the impact of injustice on resentment, it should come as no surprise that among employed wives (table 5-2) women who defined their husbands as being fair toward them report less resentment (or hostility)[7] than wives who defined their spouses' power as unfair. Further confirmation of the intimate ties between nonlegitimate power and resentment can be seen in that wives who are more persistent are more resentful. And as observed from table 5-1, the least powerful are the more persistent. Diminished power encourages a worker's persistence to try to increase her power, and the more she persists (but is only minimally successful), the more resentful she becomes.

The other side of the coin, of course, is that increased power decreases employed wives' resentment. That link can be traced not only through power's acting indirectly on resentment via persistence, but also by noting that bargaining power and resentment are negatively correlated ($r = -.30$), even though power is not able to exercise any direct path of influence on resentment. Thus, as wives perceive their husbands to have relatively less and wives to have comparatively more power, this is associated in their minds with greater justice, less continuous striving to press their demands, and less resentment.

Pervading these complex processes is the ubiquitous influence of empathy, which table 5-2 shows to be a strong predictor of lowered resentment. Recall that empathy also influenced definitions of justice, just as it had significant positive impact on wives' power. Thus wives who feel they can communicate with and be understood by husbands also experience less resentment towards them over regulated conflict. Moreover, it is vital to keep in mind that it is among better-educated, higher-status couples that empathy is most satisfactory. These couples also tend to be more sex-role-modern, with wives having greater levels of economic and intangible resources by which to chip away at husbands' power.

In that same vein, modernity on the traditional-mother-role predicts reduced resentment. Nevertheless, by way of contrast, greater egalitarianism

Table 5-2
Influences on Resentment and on Aggression, by Employment Status

Workers (n = 137)			Nonworkers (n = 184)		
Wife Resentment[a]					
	beta	r		beta	r
1975 Empathy	−.21	−.40	1975 Empathy	−.30	−.39
Persistence	+.22	.36	Status quo	+.17	.21
Husband fair	−.25	−.39	Strategy C	+.18	.23
Suppression	+.22	.32	Strategy D	+.15	.21
Status quo	+.12	.20	Husband fair	−.14	−.25
1975 IE modernity	+.14	.18	1975 PHA modernity	+.12	.13
1975 TM modernity	−.12	−.20			
Conflict-expressive	+.08*	.13			
MR = .64, R² = .42			MR = .53, ≠2 = .28		
Workers (n = 137)			Nonworkers (n = 184)		
Wife Aggression[a]					
	beta	r		beta	r
Resentment	+.33	.47	1975 Empathy	−.16	−.38
Catholic	−.25	−.29	Resentment	+.21	.37
Social class by peers	−.17	−.25	Husband-fair	−.19	−.31
Conflict-autonomy	+.20	.28	Living standard		
1975 Empathy	−.14	−.38	by peers	−.16	−.25
Strategy C	+.12	.21	Strategy B	+.16	.17
Husband-fair	−.11	−.30	Strategy C	+.13	.23
MR = .66, R² = .43			MR = .54, R² = .29		

All betas significant at .05, unless starred.
[a]Higher score = greater resentment or greater aggression.

towards husbands' behaviors results in greater resentment (just as it produced greater persistence, as shown in table 5-1). Because IE is the most radical or innovative of the seven role dimensions (figure 1-1), it—in contrast to TM—may influence wives to seek for an ever more favorable balance of power. Indeed, IE may influence wives to feel content (absence of resentment) only when genuine equality of power over this particular dispute is actually (if ever) achieved. The notion being conveyed here is similar to ideas such as "boundlessness" or "rising expectations": the more power that subordinate groups get, the more they feel they deserve (Duke, 1976). IE may indicate precisely that sort of orientation. And anything short of that ultimate goal of full equality in the sharing of power tends to generate feelings of resentment and hostility.

Finally, it turns out that both varieties of husband counterstrategies (coercion and status quo) influence wives' resentment in the expected direction. When husbands attempt to utilize suppression or nonsolutions to resolve conflicts totally in their own favor, apart from any concessions, then wives' resentment is greater. Conversely, the absence of those male strategies means reduced resentment. We saw in table 5-1 that the suppression strategy is influenced by wives' balance of power. Expanding those linkages, it may be said that reduced wife-power permits increased husband-suppression, which in turn contributes towards greater resentment. (If the wife had more power, she would get more of what she wants and "feel better" because of it.)

In short, nonlegitimate male power occurs when empathy is low and wife resources limited. Consequently, wives persist in seeking to redress their grievance and to alter the unjust balance of power. But husbands counter either by suppressing the dispute or else seeking nonsolutions uniquely favorable to husbands. One outcome of these ongoing reciprocal processes is burgeoning resentment towards husbands on the part of wives.

Resentment on the Part of Nonemployed Wives

The pattern that accounts for resentment among nonworkers is similar to that observed for workers. While IE emerged among the employed women, here among nonemployed women it is greater PHA modernity that predicts resentment. Evidently, among nonworkers, preferred concessions in husbands' behaviors as represented by PHA have the same kinds of consequences as IE did for workers—and probably for similar theoretical reasons.

Furthermore, two wife-bargaining strategies also influence resentment. If wives bargain explicitly on the basis of what they define to be right and fair (strategy D) and/or on the basis of group interests (strategy C), but discover they still cannot achieve their objectives, then the likely result is exacerbation of the kinds of negative processes Homans (1974) postulates. The data show that nonlegitimate husband-power (and concomitantly less wife-power) produces resentment by itself; and when added to that are blocked efforts to negotiate on the basis of justice and group well-being, then there are substantial increments in wife-resentment.

Aggression on the Part of Wives

Nonlegitimate power exercised by husbands during negotiations, wives' persistence to achieve their interests, husband nonsolutions, and increasing resentment on the part of wives are not likely to be without the aggression that Homans predicts. Aggression was measured using five items to which respondents could reply: "very often," "often," "sometimes," "seldom," "never."[8]

> How often does his refusal to listen, or do what you want him to do, make you so angry that:
> 1. You swear at him?
> 2. You try to hit him?
> 3. You ignore him or give him the cold shoulder?
> 4. You stamp your feet or hit something like a table or wall?
> 5. You do something to spite him?

In recent years, Straus (1976) and his colleagues have called attention to the pervasiveness of various kinds of violence in American families. Among other things, Straus has argued that there are at least three forms by which marital conflicts are resolved. (He does not discuss regulation.) These are, first, persuasion, argument, or reasoning; second, verbal aggression (that is, insults or threats, expressions of hostility); third, the use of physical force or violence.

Thus far, we have looked at the steps outlined in figure 5-1 which fit under Straus's first or reasoning category. However, when respondents use the five items listed above, conflict escalates out of form 1 (reasoning, argument, persuasion) and moves into forms 2 and 3 as outlined by Straus: verbal aggression or physical violence.

The frequency of reported active violence is relatively modest among our respondents. Eighty-six percent state that they never hit their husbands (item 2) in connection with the dispute in question, and 74 percent report "never" to item 4. (When wives were asked if their husbands ever use "physical force such as slapping, shoving, hitting or pushing" in connection with the dispute, only 12 cases responded affirmatively.) Therefore, most (not all) of the aggressive behavior that wives exhibit is captured by items 1, 3, and 5: They swear at their husbands, ignore them, give them the cold shoulder, or do something to spite them. Through factor analysis, it was found that the five items above clustered together to form a single index of aggression, which is explained in table 5-2.

Aggression on the Part of Employed Wives

It is clear that among workers, resentment is stronger than anything else in accounting for aggression.[9] Resentment is the result of the composite set of forces just discussed; and the more resentment wives have, the more aggressive they are likely to become. Ultimately, therefore, the understanding of aggression is based on all the things described above that predict resentment.

Aggression is the ultimate stage displayed in figure 5-1; and it is plain to see how variation in aggressive behavior is an outcome of this whole set of continually ongoing, and mutually reinforcing, conflict processes. In actuality, of course, aggression is not an end point but only one element embedded within those ongoing processes. Indeed, as cited above, Homans suggests that aggression may sometimes become a strategy used by aggrieved parties to assist them in ending injustice and conflict.

What are the conditions under which resentment and aggression are expressed by the aggrieved party but do not bring about actual change? And what are the conditions under which they actually do accomplish change and resolution? Unfortunately, these questions were not put to these wives. What is known is that, at the time of the interview, the dispute had not actually been resolved or "made to go away." What is not known is what effect, if any, aggression might have had on the attainment of wives' interests prior to the interview, nor what effect aggression might have had subsequent to it. What is apparent is its presence within marriage and that its variation is based on prior theoretical expectations.

A second strong influence on aggression is religion.[10] Given the greater Catholic traditionalism reported elsewhere (Scanzoni, 1975b) it should not be too surprising that Catholics report less aggression than non-Catholics. Owing both to religious and sex-role orientations, Catholic employed women appear to be more hesitant than non-Catholics to behave aggressively towards their husbands. For Catholics, to escalate aggression would be to go beyond what Blau (1964) calls the "prevailing social norms" of their religious subgroup.

The third most robust predictor of aggression is conflict over wife-autonomy. Workers who are struggling with their husbands over this highly significant area tend to engage in greater aggression than wives who dispute other issues. Indeed, of the several possible conflict areas, this is the only one that correlates significantly with aggression. Its unique link with aggression is probably due to the premise, noted previously, that it is a basic conflict. In point of fact, for women who feel strongly enough to raise the wife-autonomy issue, there is probably no issue quite as basic, nor is there a rule more fundamental to the husband-wife association.

These women seek to participate more fully in those societal trends leading to greater individualistic gratifications for women, and their husbands are resisting them. Autonomy-conflict is related to several variables, including earlier age at marriage, fewer interval months worked, greater numbers of unintended children, less education, and lower job satisfaction.[11] It thus appears that over time some less-advantaged women began to shift from their earlier traditionalism and pressed their husbands to do the same. The unwillingness and/or inability of their husbands to do so results in a chain of conflict processes that leads up to verbal and physical aggression.

Validating the growing awareness that aggression may be greater in lower-status households are several variables which, while they reveal no significant betas in influencing aggression on the part of wives towards husbands, are nevertheless correlated negatively with it: wives' fathers' job status; husbands' education, job status, and income; aggregate family income; wives' job status (r's respectively, $-.24$, $-.28$, $-.22$, $-.19$, $-.18$, $-.20$). The status variable that does influence aggression significantly is displayed in table 5-2. The higher employed wives' peers rank the social position of their households, based solely on husbands' attainments, the lower the aggression.

Throughout this and the preceding chapters, the point has been made that resources are the basis for legitimate power. And it turns out that the fairness of husbands' power has direct impact on reduced wife-aggression. Similarly, empathy exercises its own negative path of influence on aggression. The conclusion seems quite firm, therefore, that higher-status husbands who provide higher levels of both economic and expressive (empathy) rewards to wives, receive in return lower levels of aggressive-type behaviors (Gelles, 1976).

Interestingly enough, the one bargaining strategy that influences aggression positively is strategy C (the husband should do or stop doing something "because it's best for the entire family"). One might have predicted that use of this collective strategy would minimize aggression—that wives who negotiate in terms of the greater good of the whole would believe that aggression is undesirable and has negative consequences for the group. But table 4-2 revealed that strategy C is often used by less-educated women who experience less empathy, have more children, and are more TM-traditional. In other words, the polar extreme of collective strategies tends to be used by less-advantaged women.

Therefore, added to the reasons just discussed for higher aggression levels among less-advantaged households, is the kind of bargaining strategy these women use to try to resolve conflict. Presumably, strategy C is not very effective in accomplishing much change in their husbands' behavior. The appeal to the good of the whole tends not to strike husbands as enhancing their own self-interests. Therefore, being unable to effect much (if any) change, wives are more likely to become highly resentful and then aggressive.

Aggression on the Part of Nonemployed Wives

Moving to the final section of table 5-2, we find that among nonworkers, resentment is also the single most powerful influence on these wives' aggressive behaviors. Moreover, their aggression is affected by two negotiating strategies. The stronger of these is the future-oriented and individualistic bargaining strategy B (the husband should change because then the wife will do something he wants). Wives who try to negotiate on those terms, and still find their husbands intransigent, are more likely to engage in aggressive behaviors. Yet wives who bargain in terms of group interests, strategy C (the husband should change because it is in the best interests of the whole family), also tend to resort to aggression. Therefore, whether nonemployed wives opt for a collective or an individualistic strategy, neither seems very effective in bringing about as much change as they desire. Blocked bargaining strategies generate increased resentment; and as resentment builds up, it contributes to increased aggression.

Excursus: Some Possible Trends in Marital Bargaining

The theme of marital change is central to this book. Some of the indicators of such change have been shown to be whether or not work remains an option for women or comes to be defined as a right (chapter 2), whether a woman's working makes any significant differences to marriage and family patterns (chapter 3), and what is happening with regard to how women negotiate, conflict, or try to make decisions with their husbands in pressing for certain goals (chapter 4 and this chapter). As indicated in chapter 1, the theoretical expectation is that those kinds of decision processes may be expected to vary by degree of preference for gender-role differentiation.

This relates to possible trends in marital bargaining as part of basic marital change as follows: Since there is evidence that women are becoming less sex-role-traditional, and if sex roles and bargaining are associated, we can assume that the character of marital conflicts is shifting from what it was in the past. Furthermore, if sex-role preferences continue to change, we may expect continued alterations within such pivotal marriage behaviors as negotiation and conflict. These alternatives have to do with at least three items: goals, bargaining styles, and resources. Let us briefly examine each.

Goals and Interests of Wives and Husbands

When both spouses are traditional in terms of sex-role preferences, there is strong consensus over their common goals or what Coser (1956) calls the basic rules of their relationship. Both husband and wife prefer sharp sex-role differentiation, as illustrated by traditional responses to the items in figure 1-1.

However, as indicated by the data in chapter 1, some wives have become less traditional and more modern in sex-role preferences than their husbands. As a result, the potential for increased conflicts over basic rules is probably greater than it was ten, or certainly twenty-five, years ago. For instance, the incidence of women wanting to be child-free in order to pursue careers was bound to be considerably less years ago, as was the incidence of women wanting to pursue careers in other cities, commuting on weekends to be with their husbands. With such increased incidence comes potential for increased dissensus.

Styles of Bargaining

A second possible difference in conflict processes that would serve as an indicator of marital changes deals with the ways or styles that negotiation and bargaining are actually carried out. The findings of Raush et al. (1974) tend to corroborate those laboratory studies of bargaining which suggest that men and women tend to negotiate somewhat differently (Rubin and Brown, 1975).

The tentative conclusions seem to point in this direction: Men tend to be "goal-oriented," women, "reactive." Specifically, during bargaining, Opponent makes offers and counter-offers that may or may not move the two parties toward a resolution. Opponent may also make threats or otherwise engage in hostile or angry outbursts, or Opponent may attempt to coerce Actor into conformity with Opponent's demands. Actor has to try to sort out Opponent's behaviors and respond to those that will resolve the conflict, while in effect ignoring the nonproductive or merely distracting inputs. That bargaining style is called goal-oriented, and men tend to bargain that way.

Women, on the other hand, apparently tend to bargain in a more reactive fashion, which may make them less effective bargainers. That is, they tend not to sort out Opponent's productive versus nonproductive inputs. Thus, if Opponent becomes hostile, angry, or threatening, the woman may respond in kind—even though such a response may in fact impede ultimate resolution. For example, Raush et al. report that when husbands negotiate in a conciliatory manner, wives bargain that same way; but if husbands shift to a more strident style, wives shift accordingly. Rarely do husbands respond to wives' bargaining styles in quite that fashion. Instead, report Raush et al., men appear more comfortable with bargaining power than women do and seemingly know better how to use it to gain their ends.

To the degree that these tentative conclusions contain validity, they surely do not reflect any innate characteristics. Instead, they appear to be the result of the divergent socialization experiences encountered from infancy by males and females, as well as by the kinds of divergent situations in which women and men participate throughout their lives. Men are generally more active than women in the decision-making processes of religious bodies, political groups, unions, community organizations, occupations, and so forth. Therefore, men have greater opportunity to learn how to bargain effectively. Presumably, as women come to prefer less gender divergence and more role interchangeability (as indicated by modern responses to the items in figure 1-1), one of the outcomes should be greater similarity of the sexes in bargaining styles.

Already books have begun to appear advising women on how this can come about. Hennig and Jardim, for example, have pointed out how team sports help boys develop skills that later give them an advantage over women in climbing the corporate ladder. Business management, say these authors, requires hard work, determination, perseverance, "the ability to deal with criticism by seeing it as directed much less to the person and much more to task achievement" (1977:23), setting goals and objectives, aiming to win, and learning "to deal with loss by distancing it—you win some, you lose some." It also means that "one must develop a strategy that takes the environment into account. . . . How do I make use of this or counter that in order to get where I want to go?" (p. 26). Hennig and Jardim also write:

> These are personal skills. Boys begin to develop them in an outdoor classroom to which girls traditionally have had no access. After five to fifteen years of practice, men bring these skills with them to management jobs and they are skills critical to job performance once the dividing line between supervision and management is crossed. (p. 23)

The immense popularity of their book (raising it almost immediately to the *New York Times* best seller list), and the interest in the seminars these authors are holding around the country in an effort to train women in management skills, may be one more indication of coming changes in the ways women will bargain.

In addition to being less reactive and more goal-oriented, it is probable that women who are egalitarian in their sex-role preferences are less likely to be part of arrangements (including marriage arrangements) based on spontaneous consensus or implicit bargaining (compare chapter 1) and instead to become more involved in outcomes that were arrived at by explicit bargaining. The reason for that expectation is another element that appears in the bargaining literature— toughness. A tough bargainer makes high demands and grants few concessions; a soft bargainer makes few demands and grants many concessions (Bartos, 1974). By definition, therefore, tough bargainers require explicit negotiations to gain their ends. And since women in general (even the more egalitarian) are bargaining from a subordinate position, they need to be tough and thus bargain explicitly in order to achieve desired goals. Very likely, a major influence on their degree of toughness is the degree of their sex-role modernity.

Resources

Besides the range of potential disputes and also types of bargaining styles, there is a third major feature of conflict processes that can serve as an indicator of marital changes—the resources that women bring to the "bargaining table." The most obvious are tangible resources such as income. Earlier discussion referred to the finding that egalitarian women with high work continuity display relatively high earning power. The literature suggests that earning power is an important component of bargaining power. Therefore, to the degree that some women have more of the former than they did years ago, they should also currently possess more of the latter as they explicitly press for new kinds of goals and interests. But resources may also be intangible, as observed in connection with the meanings and consequences of work for women. These resources can also assist in achieving valued ends and have a crucial part to play in bargaining and conflict processes.

Summary and Conclusions

To grasp the flow of this and the preceding chapter on marital conflict and negotiation processes, it helps to think of three stages. With figure 5-1 as a guide, stage I begins with conflict-regulation and evolves through those bargaining strategies that are used most frequently. Conflict-regulation is a process that the husband does. The justice or injustice of his power in doing that is a definition ascribed to it by the wife. Whether or not she relays her grievances and the ways in which she tries to get the husband to change are reactive processes that the wife does. These male actions and wife reactions were summarized in chapter 4.

Stage II is wife-power in figure 5-1. How much can a wife get her husband to change? Trying to get more power for herself while trying simultaneously to reduce his power (getting him to change) are processes she and he do together. That simultaneous jockeying occurs during the dynamics of the bargaining processes in stage I. And that is why power is actually bargaining power. It is also why I stated repeatedly that the several concepts in figures 4-1 and 5-1 are separated from each other solely for analytic purposes. In reality, they are an intrinsic whole, constantly feeding back upon and reinforcing one another. All are subsumed under the notion of purposive action, ongoing goal-seeking, or activity aimed at achieving certain ends or outcomes. In this instance, these women want to end the dispute that their husbands currently control and replace that regulated conflict with a freshly negotiated fair exchange.

Stage III (Wife-persistence through aggression) represents what happens when wives can or cannot bring about the change they seek. In most of the literature, power is treated as an end point or outcome. Instead, figure 4-1 (and chapter 4) showed that husband-power is the cause of subsequent wife behaviors. Similarly now, degree of wife-power (figure 5-1) is the cause of subsequent actions by both partners. If the wife has less power, she is more likely to be persistent—to keep on trying to get her husband to change.

Concomitantly, having more power means she is less likely to let her husband terminate their struggle merely by suppressing it. Husbands not only attempt to do that, they also try to do nothing, that is, return the struggle to the status quo ante. Less powerful wives are less able to resist either of these husband nonsolutions. Under those circumstances, wives become extremely resentful and hostile, and they consequently act aggressively against their husbands. Whether or not the aggression becomes a means to resolution would have required a subsequent interview with these wives. It is possible that these processes could continue indefinitely or that the wife could muster enough bargaining power to replace conflict with a fair exchange. Some husbands might even succeed in suppressing further negotiations, though wives might want them, or in convincing wives to drop the negotiations entirely.

As I said in chapter 4, sex-role modernity is significant in stage I, because it generates individualistic bargaining. Egalitarian women are determined that their interests be given as much priority as those of husbands and children.

Likewise, sex-role modernity stimulates greater wife bargaining power in a variety of ways. First and foremost, egalitarian women with more tangible and intangible resources have already established a pattern of more successful negotiation. This pattern from the past does them in good stead in the present; it continues to make them more successful bargainers. Likewise, empathy increases bargaining effectiveness. And empathy is more prevalent among couples where both spouses are better-educated and therefore more gender-role modern.

Furthermore, wives with more positive empathy satisfaction are more likely to define their husbands' power as legitimate. And the more legitimate or fair or flexible that power is, the more bargaining power wives have. In effect, what is being described is a balance of power in which the balance is tipped less in the husbands' favor when wives are better-educated, sex-role modern, have both types of resources, and get empathy from their (better-educated) husbands.

Wives who lack these characteristics find the balance tipped more in their husbands' favor. Thus, they react by more constant efforts to get their husbands to change, and they are more subject to his reactions—suppression or status quo. In turn, these two husband reactions generate wife reactions of hostility and aggression.

In chapter 4, the point was made that what distinguishes the negotiations of women who hold modern gender-role preferences is their concern for their own well-being—their individualistic rights. In this chapter, we find that this same concern for self-interest is related to the amount of bargaining power these women are actually able to exercise. When it comes to the subsequent processes represented by stage III, two themes emerge. Some egalitarian (and more powerful) women are under less pressure to persist, to face husband nonsolutions, to become resentful and aggressive. But on the other hand, some must endure all of these phenomena. For example, certain women who specifically expect changes in their husbands' own role behaviors are also more likely to keep on pressing for even greater change than they have already accomplished, and to be more resentful when it does not occur.

The key to this divergence would seem to be their husbands' gender-role modernity and negotiating flexibility. Gender-modern women married to comparably egalitarian men are less likely to experience those unpleasant post-power processes. Gender-modern women married to gender-traditional men, on the other hand, seem most likely to have to cope with them.

As argued throughout this book, in the years ahead younger women are likely to continue developing increasingly egalitarian sex-role preferences and to gain greater levels of both tangible and intangible resources. Work is likely to become defined ever more strongly as their inherent right, as assessed by indicators such as those utilized in chapter 2. The significance of employment for such women should continue to grow beyond the levels documented in chapter 3, in terms of its impacts on family lifestyle and social-class position and in terms of its impact on the status of household provider. That status should gradually cease to be the exclusive domain of males.

As these changes become more widespread, women are increasingly likely to develop interests or goals that much more frequently than now run counter to husbands' interests. One outgrowth of that will be the continual undermining of the spontaneous consensus (wives are "supposed" to do this; husbands are "supposed" to do that) which in the past has led many wives to defer without much thought to husbands' interests. Unfair exchanges will simultaneously become more common yet less acceptable, and thus wives will want to bargain with greater frequency and toughness. The trend toward younger wives wanting to establish more equitable bargaining positions seems clear and inexorable (compare Goode, 1966:506).

Nevertheless, it can be posited that, over time, as wives gain greater bargaining power and find themselves just as able as husbands to maintain regulated disputes, such conflicts may in effect tend to cancel each other out. That is, as husbands experience the reality of having to deal with what they consider nonlegitimate power and unfair exchanges that their wives impose on them, husbands may come to perceive that their own greatest utility is gained by agreeing to compromises over the specific areas where they themselves exercise nonlegitimate power. Since they desire to be rid of inequities they experience, husbands may conclude the most feasible way to do that is to remove inequities perceived by wives. Thus, wives' greater capabilities to generate regulated conflicts could eventually result in shorter time spans for such disputes, and the emergence (for women) of greater numbers of fair exchanges than currently exist.

These matters speak to a fundamental theoretical issue raised in chapters 4 and 5: individual versus group interests, and consequences for group solidarity and maintenance. Divorce rates have risen and may once again rise, owing in part to increases in sex-role modernity among women and wives' resultant increased determination to achieve fair exchanges in marriages.

But that divorce trend is not necessarily inexorable. Recent data, for instance, show that over the past several years divorce rates have been gradually leveling off (U.S.D.H.E.W., 1977).

The greater the numbers of women who attain resources that increase their bargaining power, the fewer the number of alternative traditional-type "sellers" who will be available to men in the marriage market. The pool of powerless women on whom men can more or less impose regulated conflicts will have decreased and, in contrast to the present, men will be forced to bargain with women relatively as powerful as they. If, as suggested above, one outcome is a greater frequency of fair exchanges, then the incidence of group terminations could possibly decline. Thus, in the long run, individualistic interests may contribute to increased group solidarity, once the formerly dominant party becomes convinced that it has no more viable (more profitable) alternative but to stay and negotiate.

Notes

1. See chapter 4.
2. "Yes" = 64 percent; "no" = 36 percent.
3. See chapter 3, note 18.
4. "Yes" = 25 percent; "no" = 75 percent.
5. "Yes" = 37 percent; "no" = 63 percent.
6. See chapter 4, note 2, for explanation of budget skills.
7. "When he does not listen to the reasons you give or else does nothing about it, do you resent that: strongly (34 percent), somewhat (33 percent), a little (23 percent), or not at all (10 percent)?"
8. Percentage distributions of five response categories, respectively, were: *item one*—2, 10, 27, 23, 38; *item two*—0, 2, 4, 8, 86; *item three*—5, 11, 35, 22, 27; *item four*—1, 3, 11, 11, 74; *item five*—2, 5, 16, 19, 58.
9. Resentment explains 22 percent of the variance.
10. The measure of "religion" is Catholics vs. non-Catholics. This was the procedure followed in Scanzoni, 1975b. While I recognize that some non-Catholics may be as sex-role-traditional as Catholics, that distinction did not emerge simply by separating non-Catholics by denominational labels (Baptists, etc.). In short, in order to discover differences that religion makes, one needs more than denominational labels. Since such information was not available to us, we followed Ryder and Westoff (1971) in making this dichotomy. Further research into religion and gender differentiation would require more sensitive measures such as doctrinal positions, and so forth.
11. r's respectively = −.21, −.16, −.26, −.14, −.24.

6
Summary and Policy Implications

"The more things change the more they stay the same" is an old saying that might apply to some things such as palace revolutions or presidential elections. But democracies are not the same as monarchies, rigid caste societies are different from open class systems, and societies that maintained the institution of slavery differed from those that got rid of it. In all three instances, change from what was to what emerged was profound. All of them represented the extension of basic rights, privileges, and opportunities to include ever-widening sectors of humankind.

Similarly, the inclusion of women under the umbrella of these rights and privileges also marks significant social change. Societies where these extensions are taking place are different from those where they are absent. Inevitably, such changes affect marriage and family institutions profoundly.

Prior chapters considered three fundamental changes in these institutions associated with opening up the opportunity structure to women. These include the evolutionary movement in the meaning of work from option to right; the gradual shift from women's work having minimal impacts to having considerable structural consequences for marriage and family; and the movements from spontaneous consensus and women negotiating primarily for group well-being to women negotiating for individual well-being.

The point was made that increases in the proportion of women in the paid labor force is by itself no indicator of fundamental family change. It is probable, of course, that long-term increases in labor-force activity have been associated with these (and other) kinds of familial changes. Very likely, over the past six or seven decades, women's work involvement and these kinds of changes have mutually reinforced one another through ongoing feedback.

Reward-Cost Theory

To help organize, understand, and explain these substantive changes, I used an eclectic version of reward-cost theory. Subsumed under this rubric are essential elements of exchange and conflict theories, along with approaches labeled variously in the literature as power, resource, utilitarian, purposive action, and so forth. Central to all of these perspectives is the idea of goal-seeking. Persons hold preferences, goals, interests, objectives, and rewards that they desire or want to attain. As applied to marriage and family, the argument was that women and men vary in the degree to which they want or prefer traditional gender differentiation to continue. To prefer gender differentiation is to prefer certain rewards and to be willing for or indifferent to costs associated with it. Conversely, to prefer gender equality or interchangeability is to want rewards and be indifferent to or willing for costs associated with that sort of situation.

Sex-Role Preferences

To measure these preferences several sex-role dimensions were utilized. These particular sex-role dimensions are part of a growing literature suggesting that over the last several years there has been a noticeable shift in the direction of more widespread and stronger preferences for gender equality. For instance, the women in this sample showed significant increases between 1971 and 1975 in their own preferences for sex-role modernity. The point that there is a gradual shift away from preferences for traditional gender differentiation is pivotal because on that is hung the three sets of changes described in prior chapters.

Meanings of Work

Take, for example, the question of whether women define their work as option or as right. Several sets of indicators of work-meaning were presented and analyzed. These include intangible resources, occupational achievement orientations, career definitions and preferences, occupational satisfactions, husbands' geographic mobility on wife's behalf, and priorities held for her own as opposed to husband and child priorities. Women who rank "high" or "strong" on these dimensions were said to view their paid employment as a right; those who rank lower are more likely to view it as merely an option. It turns out that women who hold modern or egalitarian sex-role preferences are more likely to rank high on these several dimensions.

In short, the more sex-role-egalitarian women are, the more likely they are to view paid employment as a right. Furthermore, since it appears that greater numbers of women are more strongly sex-role-egalitarian now than was the case ten or twenty years ago, it is therefore quite probable that more women currently view work as a right than was true years ago. More specifically, more women today than ever before are very likely to rank high on the several indicators of the meaning of work, and thus to be defining it as a right.

Consequences of Work

Corresponding to changes in work's meanings are changes in work's consequences or impacts. Some women do perceive and believe that their working enhances the living standard that their family is able to enjoy, and also that it enhances the social class position of their households. Furthermore, there is a strong correspondence between what these women perceive and what they believe significant others (friends, relatives) perceive. In short if they believe their working has significant impact on their family's lifestyle and social class position, they are likely to be reinforced in those convictions by others in their social network.

Once again, women who hold modern sex-role preferences more strongly are more likely to report those kinds of positive and far-reaching social consequences. When, in the past, larger numbers of women were more strongly sex-role-traditional, those impacts were rarely if ever felt. But an increase in the numbers of women who are more strongly sex-role-modern signals change because those kinds of consequences therefore become more common than they were years or decades ago.

Resources

Simultaneously, while preferences or goals are intrinsic to any version of reward-cost theory, so is the matter of resources. It was quite apparent, for instance, that tangible resources (namely their own earnings) contribute greatly both to enhanced family lifestyle and to social class position. Their intangible resources (skills and capabilities pertinent to goal-attainment both in the occupational and familial realms; compare figure 2-1) aided in similar and substantial fashion. It turns out that our measures of sex roles are also highly correlated with both types of resources.

Therefore, the argument was made that the three kinds of factors (preferences, tangible and intangible resources) represent a sort of syndrome in which over the years, the several elements mutually reinforce and feed back on one another. For instance, women who prefer individualistic goals (that is, sex-role egalitarianism) also tend to have greater levels of resources which make goal attainment that much more possible; and thus in turn that attainment presumably strengthens their individualistic preferences. In short, familial changes are not accomplished merely through preferences for egalitarianism. While those sorts of preferences seem to be requisite, they are not sufficient. What are both necessary and sufficient to accomplish changes are preferences and resources.

Coprovider Status

That three-part syndrome was clearly observed operating in terms of the third consequence of women's employment, namely, modification of the family-provider status. Formerly the unique province of males, some women workers in the sample see themselves as coproviders, cooccupants of that status. They see themselves sharing that duty with their husbands. And that sort of interchangeability occurs when women are high both in resources and strong in egalitarian sex-role preferences.

Furthermore, provider interchangeability stimulates greater husband participation in childcare duties. Concomitantly, resources and sex-role preferences increase husband participation in other household tasks such as cooking and dishwashing. Thus, the more wives achieve interchangeability in being household providers (and the more egalitarian they are and the more resources they have), the more it appears that they can also get their husbands to become more interchangeable with them in the performance of strictly domestic duties.

As was the case for the two prior consequences, household-role interchangeability was probably rarer years ago. Presumably, however, it has in recent years become more common as sex-role preferences have shifted in a more egalitarian direction.

Two caveats should be attached to conclusions about these three sets of consequences. First, by no means are men as heavily involved in domestic duties as are women. We are talking about relative male participation according to whether or not the wife works, how egalitarian she is, and how great are her resources.

Second, compared to men, the impacts of women's earnings are currently limited because women's earnings have been limited. Owing to the effects of stereotypical gender socialization, as well as discrimination, women's continuity (frequency of labor-force involvement) has generally been less than that of men's. However, unfolding trends regarding women's income were considered in chapter 3; and what the prospects might be for the future are considered below.

Negotiation, Conflict, and Power

The final set of changes examined in prior chapters revolved around women's negotiation and conflict behaviors, or what Duke (1976) has labeled processes of decision making. I just observed that intrinsic to reward-cost theory are both preferences (desired goals) and resources. Equally central and inherent are the processes whereby persons or groups actually use or manipulate available resources in order to realize their goals—either wholly or in part.

Because of the great reliance of contemporary sociology on cross-sectional surveys we tend to ignore the realities of goal-oriented processes. At point 1 in time certain wives, for instance, hold preferences regarding goals they want from their husbands. Wives also hold resources to help attain those goals. By point 2 women have realized some, all, or none of those goals. In between points 1 and 2 they have either negotiated explicitly and/or conflicted with their husbands, or, else bargained implicitly and/or concurred with them on the basis of spontaneous consensus. In large part because those processes are extremely difficult to conceptualize and measure, sociologists in recent decades have overlooked them.

Chapters 4 and 5 are one initial effort to explore these complex processes outside the laboratory in actual settings. Respondents reported an issue that was conceptualized as regulated conflict. That is, husbands were demonstrating greater power than wives over this particular dispute by maintaining the status quo against their will or desires. I then explored certain aspects of how women subsequently negotiate with their husbands to try to get them to change. It turned out that sex-role preferences were quite significant in affecting negotiating styles. Traditional women tended to try to persuade their husbands to change by arguing on the basis of family (group) well-being. Conversely, egalitarian women were more likely to argue for change on the basis of individualistic concerns or self-interest.

Besides sex-role modernity, their resources (tangible and intangible) had predictable impacts on bargaining style: the more resources they had the more individualistic was their bargaining. Simultaneously, other factors from prior chapters also influenced the results. Specifically, women who ranked higher on several of the indicators that showed working is a right were generally less likely to bargain on the basis of group well-being. Similarly, women who perceived that their working enhanced family living standard and social class position were also less likely to bargain in traditional fashion, or in terms of group interests. Interchangeability in the performance of household duties tended to produce similar results, namely, less traditional bargaining.

In analogous fashion, when we probed how much bargaining power these wives had, that is, how successful they were in actually getting their husbands to change, similar findings emerged. Egalitarian sex roles and greater resources, plus decisions from prior chapters explained by egalitarian preferences and greater resources, tended to account for greater wife-power.

In short, the more egalitarian wives are and the more resources they possess, the more likely they are to bargain on the basis of self-interest; what is more, such wives are likely to be more effective bargainers in terms of getting more of what they want. And once again, since sex roles appear to be shifting, such bargaining patterns represent changes from patterns that predominated years ago. When sex-role preferences were more traditional and women had fewer resources (especially tangible), if they negotiated at all they were more likely to do so in terms of what was best for the children, the family, and the group as a whole. Very often there may have been little explicit negotiation, but instead a high frequency of implicit understandings as to the distribution of responsibilities and rights.

Implications of Work for Marital Conflict

And as long as women did not view work as one of their rights; and as long as their relatively noncontinuous labor-force participation did not affect familial structural patterns, there was comparatively less likelihood of a great number of serious regulated conflicts over the basic rules of their relationship. When there were conflicts, say, over how to spend his income, her negotiating strategies were presumably based on group well-being: "It's best for the kids to buy X rather than Y." As long as women (and men) preferred that sharp differentiation between domestic and occupational spheres, women had little reason to negotiate for any autonomous or independent benefits. If the family group did well, she did well too.

But with growing preferences for role interchangeability, along with concomitant changes in the meanings of work as well as its consequences, the woman's own interests, autonomy, and independence become more prominent and salient than ever before. As discussed in chapters 1, 4, and 5, areas that had rarely ever been questioned now become potentially disputable issues. Concomitantly, women's negotiating styles become gradually transformed. They begin to press for deals, outcomes, or bargains that they consider equitable to their own interests. They become what is known in the negotiation literature as tough bargainers. Their approach to family decision making, in contrast to the stance described above for traditional wives, is that if they (wives) do well then the family group will too. I will discuss the policy implications of this increasingly less subtle but all-important shift later in the chapter.

Significance of Social Processes

It can be argued that no other single issue is more important to contemporary sociology in general than the conceptualization and measurement of these kinds of decision processes. The heritage of sociology via Simmel, Marx, and Weber was centered in the study of processes (Duke, 1976). Building on Simmel, the first and extraordinarily influential sociology textbook made the point that it is out of these processes that patterns or structures arise (Park and Burgess, 1921). Functionalism, as applied throughout sociology, took the focus off the sources of patterns, and instead led us to believe that the patterns themselves were somehow virtually immutable. Spiegel (1957), for instance, creates this impression with regard to patterns of marital sex role differentiation. However, as noted in chapter 1, Coser (1976) observes that that functionalist view of social reality is being "eclipsed" in favor of a return to the much earlier stress on process.

A recent and influential work by Collins (1975:89) restates the Park and Burgess assertion in contemporary idiom:

> . . . Social structures . . . are empirically nothing more than [persons] meeting and communicating in certain ways. . . . [Persons] are continually recreating social organization. Social change is what happens when the balance of resources slips one way or another so that the relations [persons] negotiate over and over again come out in changed form.

The significance of a "process view" of social reality for any kind of change, including marital change, is quite apparent. Change is neither mysterious nor random. It emerges out of the conjoint "purposive actions" of two or more parties who have interests or goals that diverge to a greater or lesser extent. To try to reconcile those differences the parties engage in some sorts of negotiations and/or conflicts the outcomes of which are new or changed patterns, as discussed in chapters 4 and 5.

In short, the prime arena from whence springs social changes in marriage and family patterns would appear to be these conflict and negotiation processes. Presumably, the kinds of changes that have already occurred up through the 1970s are ultimately the result of these processes. Furthermore, the changes that are occurring right now emerge in the same ways; and future changes can be expected to do likewise.

Inherent within that arena of negotiation or decision-making processes are preferences for certain goals, tangible and intangible resources, and the meanings of work in terms of its several indicators, along with the consequences of women's work. (Surely contextual factors not considered in prior pages must enter in as well.) And it is through decision-making processes that linkages are established and maintained among all these numerous elements. For example, recall that the several sex-role dimensions are measuring preferences for continued differentiation or else interchangeability. The preferences are realized through these processes. When interchangeability is the goal, the processes and the elements that are intrinsic to them (resources, work meanings and consequences, and so on) operate in one fashion. But where differentiation is the goal those processes and their intrinsic elements operate in quite another fashion. Therefore the structural outcome, that is, the degree of actual behavioral marital/familial gender differentiation may be said to be caused by, the result of, or the effect of those processes.

Significance of Males

Implicit throughout the book is the Marxian/Weberian notion that since women are the subordinate group, they may be presumed to be the ones who have more often pressed for significant changes through negotiation/conflict processes. Elsewhere (1979d) I have argued that over the last 200 years this female pressure has probably been growing into an increasingly overt feature of marriage. Given the current renaissance of feminism and the greater legitimacy of pursuing individualistic preferences, female pressures for equity and justice have become more overt and "up front." For example, among the recent spate of books and articles on women's assertiveness, several contain sections devoted to developing skills in the uses of bargaining power (compare Butler, 1976:268-300).

The conclusion that perhaps the most significant feature of contemporary marriage is the evolution of tough negotiations generated by and beneficial to women in no way excludes the importance of men's negotiating behaviors. Quite the contrary, these trends among women underscore the absolute necessity to investigate men's negotiating behaviors, as well as women's. After all it is out of their necessarily joint efforts to negotiate that new arrangements emerge pertaining to occupational behaviors, childbearing, childcare, consumption, nonwork activities, sexual styles, and so forth.

Unfortunately, limited funds made it impossible to interview husbands in 1975, and so the preceding chapters had to rely solely on the reports of wives. But there is no methodological reason why future studies of processes could not include husbands as well.

As observed in chapter 1, sociology's classic concerns have been with group emergence, persistence, change, and dissolution. All four of these questions are relevant to marriage and family qua group. All of them can be attacked from the process or purposive-action perspectives described above. But for these four group questions to be researched most validly, data are required from both group partners, in other words, both spouses, whether the data are obtained by interview, observation, or some multi-method approach.

Substantive Propositions

Besides the preceding discussion and earlier chapter summaries, it is possible to condense the major findings in the form of the following systematically interrelated propositions. In doing so, a great deal of subtlety, detail and qualification are lost, but what is gained, of course, is a general and integrated overview of the study's main thrusts. Therefore, while depth and ambiguities are sacrificed, one's grasp of the major findings is increased significantly. The reader will recognize that points 1 through 5, while discussed in prior chapters, were not in this report the main foci of explanation. However, since they do figure prominently in the explanation of subsequent relationships, and since they have been accounted for elsewhere, they are included here.

1. The higher the parental status, the higher the daughter's (woman's) education.
2. The higher the parental status and woman's education, the greater her gender modernity.
3. The greater her gender modernity, the greater her postmarital work involvement over time.
4. The greater her gender modernity and work involvement, the greater her income production (tangible resources) over time.
5. The greater her gender modernity and the lower her birth intentions, the fewer children she has over time.

6. The greater her parent's education, her own education, and her gender modernity, the greater her level of intangible external resources.
   a. The greater the level of external resources, the greater the level of intangible internal resources.
7. The greater her education, gender modernity, income production, and external resources, then:
   a. The stronger her occupational achievement orientations;
   b. The greater the importance of her occupation relative to her husband's occupation and to children;
   c. The more likely she is to be career-oriented and job-satisfied;
   d. The more likely she is to obtain husband geographic-mobility relative to her occupation.
8. The greater the woman's gender modernity, external resources, and income production, and the lower her husband's material resources, the greater her positive impact on the household in terms of enhanced living standard and social class position.
9. The greater her income production, work involvement, and gender modernity, and the lower her husband's material resources, the more likely she is to occupy the status of coprovider with her husband.
10. The greater her income production, gender modernity, and intangible resources, and the more she shares coprovider duties, the more likely she is to have her husband share domestic duties.
11. The greater her gender-role modernity, the fewer children she has, and the greater her internal resources, the more likely she is to negotiate on the basis of individualistic rather than group-oriented strategies in order to seek to resolve ongoing conflict.
12. The more successfully she had negotiated her husband into sharing certain household duties in the past the more legitimate she perceives his power to be, and the more gender-role modern she is, the more bargaining power she possesses.

While these twelve propositions subsume many of the study's findings, two variables not explicit in these propositions are economic satisfactions and empathy. Economic satisfactions influence empathy positively, and the latter is significant in helping to account for many of the conflict processes analyzed in chapters 4 and 5.

But overall, these propostions summarize the main thrust of the book. They assume a temporal sequence or ongoing flow, commencing with the woman's family of origin, extending onward through her marriage, her ongoing work involvement, her ongoing fertility behavior, and her ongoing struggles with her husband to attain her interests—to make possible equitable situations both within the household and outside of it. Central to these propostions, and pervading every aspect of them, are sex-role preferences which are by no means static. There seems little doubt that over the years those preferences are affected by many of the features present in these propositions. Indeed, as suggested throughout prior chapters, there is very likely continual, complex, ongoing feedback between those features and sex-role preferences.

Future Prospects

Throughout the book the argument was made that we may continue to expect greater numbers of (younger) women to develop increasingly egalitarian sex-role preferences. Younger men can be expected to do likewise, but at a slower pace. We may also expect that, in spite of current disparities, women's earnings (tangible resources) should become comparable to those of men, but only where work continuity has been similar throughout all of their adult lives. Besides younger persons emerging as more sex-role-modern is the likelihood that increasing numbers of persons (women especially) in their thirties and forties who had formerly been quite traditional will begin to develop preferences for egalitarian goals.

These egalitarian trends appear as entrenched within modern societies as preferences by blacks for full economic equality. Neither set of aspirations, it seems to me, can be effectively squelched; although both the Black and Women's Movements often suffer setbacks, and both proceed at a very slow, gradual, and evolutionary pace. Therefore, as evolution towards gender egalitarianism continues, so also may we expect the phenomena described in this book to become increasingly salient and significant. (Compare Knudsen, 1975, for a different viewpoint.)

On the several indicators of the meaning of work, for instance, greater numbers of women can be expected to rank more toward the work-as-right end of the continuum. The impact of women's working on critical family patterns is likely to become ever more emphatic, clear cut, and far reaching than at present. Simultaneously, women's bargaining strategies are likely to become increasingly effective in terms of gaining their own interests. In essence, their bargaining power is likely to become greater continually.

Social Policy

Given these projections about trends that are likely to continue into the foreseeable future, what are the policy implications to be drawn in order to maximize prospects for familial and societal well-being at the same time that individual interests are being attained?

The major policy or quality-of-life theme that underlies this entire volume is what Gerson describes as "the ancient problem of balancing off the good of the individual and the good of society-as-a-whole" (1976:797). Gerson argues that an individualistic conception of the quality of life is based on "the degree to which an individual succeeds in accomplishing his desires despite the constraints put upon him" by his social milieu (p. 794). Conversely, what he labels a "transcendental" or collectivist approach to the quality of life is based on "the degree to which a person carries out his place in the larger social order" (p. 795).

However, Gerson also points out, as does Ellis (1971), that "the distinction between the two is merely one of shift in frame of reference, the one taking individuals as standpoint, the other taking settings and groups of settings as standpoints" (p. 799). The compatibility of individual and group interests is brought about, claims Gerson, by negotiations that result in both "individual satisfaction" and "commitment flow among settings." The latter idea simply refers to group loyalty, or behavior that promotes the good of the whole. While the compatibility of the two sets of interests is achieved when stable patterns of organization promote optimal individual interests, Gerson says "we would expect compatibility to be a rather rare event" (p. 799). Instead, he concludes, clashes among "classes of individuals" and between individual and group interests are much more common.

These issues were wrestled with explicitly in chapters 4 and 5 and are implicit in other chapters. My theme has been change—change from one set of stable patterns of marital/familial organization (differentiation) to another set of still-emerging patterns (interchangeability). Presumably, the change is being brought about because an increasing minority of women see their satisfactions minimized by the former patterns, and maximized by the latter. Government policy, at least in terms of women's employment, has recently been indirectly supportive of these kinds of changes. But following Gerson's logic, the question is: are the changes beneficial to the political system, the economic system, and to other aspects of the larger society, that is, to order and stability in general? And how do the changes benefit the other interest groups most affected by them—husbands, dependent children, and those traditional women and men who prefer gender differentiation?

Social Order

It is a commonly heard argument that these kinds of changes may contribute towards increases in marital dissolution. However, as Goode (1966) and others have argued, the divorce rate by itself cannot be taken as an indicator that social order is being threatened. Instead, the "safety-valve" view of divorce suggests that social order is actually preserved by allowing persons simple escape from costly situations. Were such escape not possible, family systems might indeed become convulsed. The argument is not that divorce is not painful to persons involved, but merely that it does not appear to pose the sort of threat to social order as defined by Gerson, that is, persons behaving contrary to transcendental ends, or against the good of the whole.

In short, most women still desire to establish relationships with men called "marriage" (and if divorced or widowed, to remarry) and to have at least one offspring, thus establishing "family." Moreover, as both spouse and mother, most women appear to be bargaining in good faith. They want to make inputs into husband and child that are beneficial to both; they do not wish to exploit. Therefore, if, in the midst of all the changes described in this book (as well as those beyond its scope), these kinds of collectivist or transcendental goals are being maintained (and there seems to be every indication that they are, Scanzoni and Scanzoni, 1976), then neither family nor social order are being undermined. Indeed, the argument can and has been made that emerging patterns will promote family and social order more fully than traditional patterns (Holter, 1970).[1]

For instance, the most obvious benefit to the larger society of the increasing emphasis on woman's individualism is the releasing of the pool of previously hidden resources which are made available to institutions of government, economy, education, basic and applied science, religion, the arts, in other words, Plato's ancient dream. Like blacks, women have constituted a reservoir of talent that, once impediments to its flow are minimized, can potentially benefit all these institutions, and thus all persons in society.

Husbands

Benefits to husbands are subsumed under the Fogarty et al. (1971) notion of "colleague." Their argument is that within the coprovider or equal-partner arrangement women can provide men with higher levels of both intangible and tangible benefits, than can traditional wives. That such efforts at higher inputs by women to men should, for a period of time, contribute to sharp conflicts and increased marital dissolution rates can be attributed to a variety of factors. Perhaps most central of these is that most men do not yet define the new arrangements as more profitable than the old—they perceive net loss rather than the net gain perceived by an increasing proportion of women.

Potentially, one of the most profound benefits that both men and women can reap from egalitarian or symmetrical marriage forms is increases in what the historian Gadlin (1974) calls "intimate relations." That term is equivalent to what elsewhere has been called the expressive or emotional side of marriage.

In tracing the history of marital intimacy, Gadlin focuses first on the colonial period where women were the property of their husbands. "Social status serves as a mold within which the contents of intimacy are shaped. Social status therefore provides limits to the meaning of intimacy. . . . When men and women have different status in society, their personal relations have different meanings to each" (p. 12). His point is that as long as husband and wife were owner and property, there may have been a great deal of respect between them, perhaps even affection, but inevitably their fundamental inequality made deep intimacy and genuine friendship virtually impossible to attain.

Gadlin goes on to argue that with the nineteenth century evolution of marriage into what elsewhere (Scanzoni, 1972) I called wife as complement, and then with the twentieth-century evolution into wife as junior partner,[2] social status inequalities between the sexes began to decline. With that decline came possibilities for greater intimacy in the form of genuine friendship and sexual enjoyment for both partners. So that while gradually increasing equality of the sexes may have resulted in long-term increases in divorces and divorce rates, it also resulted in more satisfactory marriages among those who stayed married or who had remarried.

Gadlin then comes to the contemporary era, or what I labeled the emergence of the equal-partner (coprovider) phenomenon. "Clearly, a social structure does not guarantee the actualization of persons. Certainly, the elimination of economic and sexual inequality . . . is not the same as satisfying, passionate, and loving relations. But I cannot believe that such relations are possible between people who are not free to be equals" (p. 54). In short, Gadlin contends that the equal-partner marriage, with negotiation for justice at its core, has the potential for supplying a greater depth of marital intimacy for both sexes than has ever before been possible.

In earlier chapters I referred to at least two additional gains for males besides intimacy benefits. One is the higher standard of living to which the equal-partner wife contributes for the benefit of husband (and any children) and well as herself. In an era of inflation and economic uncertainty, this type of gratification may become increasingly significant to younger males.

A second benefit is the greater labor-force flexibility that an equal partner can potentially offer a man. While the ramifications of this possibility have yet to be explored, it would seem that when women are equally responsible for household provision, men could conceivably have a greater range of choices regarding work than they do at present. These choices might include greater willingness to take certain risks—to shift jobs within a particular occupational category or to change one's type of job entirely, go/return to school, exit from the labor force for a time, "experiment" with a business of one's own, and so forth. While some men currently do these things, many others might wish to but do not out of fear of negative economic consequences. The presence of a coprovider could significantly allay those kinds of fears.

We hear a great deal, for example, about men "caught" or "trapped" in occupations that no longer provide meaning or challenge, if indeed they ever did. While having a coprovider is by no means a panacea or the "total solution" to such complex problems, it could perhaps in some cases be one part of the solution. Men in such situations might be more willing to take necessary risks to leave those situations if a coprovider were present. Incidentally, this kind of possibility could perhaps appeal just as strongly to some blue collar and lower-middle-class men as it might to upper-middle-class men. Such a strategy might be one way to win the sympathies of less-educated men who up to this point have been least amenable to women's changing aspirations.

The reverse, of course, is linked to our discussion in chapter 2 regarding men's willingness to follow women to another locale so that women can pursue their own occupations. That could be costly to men as could the situation where a man might want to move elsewhere in order to seize a job opportunity but his wife would not because of her own occupational interests. Clearly there are no pat answers to these complex issues. The only way they can be approached is in a context of negotiation for justice, or desire for maximum joint profit.

However, as long as most men define arrangements based on genuine interchangeability in childcare, household chores, and occupational endeavors as inimical to their own best interests, then the potential for increased marital conflict and dissolution remains high. Nevertheless, we learned that some men are willing to maintain what their wives view as relatively egalitarian marriages. Moreover, chapter 1 supplied evidence that younger men are more gender-role-modern than older men. Therefore, a reasonable expectation is that in the future an increasing proportion of men is likely to be negotiated into these emerging arrangements precisely because they will have come to define them as holding more maximum joint profit than do traditional forms.

Children

Dependent children, unlike husbands, cannot easily extricate themselves from unprofitable situations, and thus some observers have expressed concern for their interests in the midst of these evolutionary changes. Chapter 3 reviewed recent literature suggesting that children in day-care centers are not harmed when compared to children who were with their mothers. However, much more research is needed to probe the relative costs and benefits of every type of childcare setting.

For instance, one crucial cost identified by critics of traditional marriage patterns needs to be taken quite seriously. They contend that in those arrangements, boys learn to be instrumental or task-oriented, but they are not sufficiently trained to be expressive, or person-oriented (Balswick and Peek, 1971). Similarly, girls learn to be expressive but grow up lacking in the instrumental dimension (Scanzoni, 1975b). For children, one of the presumed beneficial outcomes of equal-partner arrangements, in which men are supposedly more involved in childcare, is what some have called "androgyny." Hopefully, boys would learn to balance task-orientation with greater person-orientation; girls would learn to balance person-orientation with greater task-orientation.

Simultaneously, one must not lose sight of the fact that childrearing is not something from which children alone profit (and suffer). There is a whole literature describing its benefits (and costs) to parents—especially mothers.[3] Equal-partner arrangements would make more of those benefits (and costs) available to fathers than is possible under lifestyles in which they are sole or chief breadwinner.

Traditional Persons

Finally (following Gerson's discussion), what about the quality of life for women (and men) who prefer traditional arrangements? Are their interests being met; and if so, will they continue to be met into the future as their proportion gradually decreases? The policy issue is the level at which governments, schools, businesses, churches, media, organized sports, and so forth, should promote gender egalitarianism in general, and equal-partner marriages in particular. While some may argue that that support level remains minimal, compared to the early 1960s it has increased significantly. And, in all probability, major institutions will continue to increase those support levels slowly but steadily.

Nevertheless, in the face of these seemingly inexorable social trends, all groups and individuals must be able to maintain options, or freedoms, or what Gerson calls "sovereignties" to define for themselves what quality of life means for them. The relative costs and rewards of various types of marriage arrangements,[4] and related occupational efforts, should be researched thoroughly, and that information widely disseminated to single as well as married persons. On the basis of that information, parents would be better able to decide consciously how they might wish to try to socialize their own children. Similarly, adults could decide more intelligently than they are currently able to do where (during any stage of their lives) they might prefer to be on the continuum of marriage-arrangements, ranging from complement to junior-partner to equal-partner.

Notes

1. For an example of this emerging theme in the media, see *Working Woman*, February, 1977, *passim*, especially an essay by Stella Chase, p. 5.

2. The junior-partner marriage arrangement is analogous to what was described in chapter 2, namely, the woman works for pay outside the home, but considers it essentially an option not a right. Also, in terms of chapter 3, she does not define herself as coprovider with her husband. (See Scanzoni, 1972.) The complement type is what was referred to in earlier chapters as the nonworking wife.

3. See Scanzoni and Scanzoni, 1976.

4. Complement, junior-partner, equal-partner.

References

Balswick, Jack O., and Peek, Charles W.
  1971   The inexpressive male: A tragedy of American society. *The Family Coordinator* 20:363-368.
Bane, Mary Jo.
  1976   *Here to Stay: American Families in the Twentieth Century.* New York: Basic Books.
Bartos, Otomar J.
  1974   *Process and Outcomes of Negotiations.* New York: Columbia University Press.
Bayer, Alan E.
  1975   Sexist students in American colleges: A descriptive note. *Journal of Marriage and Family* 37:391-400.
Bendix, Reinhard.
  1962   *Max Weber: An Intellectual Portrait.* New York: Doubleday.
Blau, Francine D.
  1975   "Longitudinal patterns of female labor force participation." In *Dual Careers: A Longitudinal Analysis of the Labor Market Experience of Women.* Vol. 4. Columbus: Center for Human Resource Research, Ohio State University, pp. 27-55.
Blau, Peter M.
  1964   *Exchange and Power in Social Life.* New York: Wiley.
Blau, Peter M., and Dudley, Otis.
  1967   *The American Occupational Structure.* New York: Wiley.
Bem, Sandra L.
  1977   On the utility of alternative procedures for assessing psychological androgyny. *Journal of Consulting and Clinical Psychology* 45:196-205.
Brickman, Phillip.
  1974   *Social Conflict.* Lexington, Mass.: D.C. Heath.
Burke, R.J., and Weir, T.
  1976   Relationship of wife's employment status to husband, wife and pair satisfaction and performance. *Journal of Marriage and Family* 38:279-287.
Butler, P.E.
  1976   *Self-Assertion for Women.* San Francisco: Canfield Press.
Chadwick-Jones, J.K.
  1976   *Social Exchange Theory: Its Structure and Influence in Social Psychology.* New York: Academic Press.
Chertkoff, J.M., and Esser, J.K.
  1976   A review of experiments in explicit bargaining. *Journal of Experimental Social Psychology* 12:464-486.

163

Coleman, James S.
  1975   "Social structure and a theory of action." In Blau, P.M., ed. *Approaches to the Study of Social Structure.* New York: Free Press, pp. 76-93.
Collins, Randall.
  1975   *Conflict Sociology.* New York: Academic Press.
Coser, Lewis A.
  1956   *The Functions of Social Conflict.* New York: Free Press.
Coser, Lewis A.
  1976   Sociological theory from the Chicago dominance to 1965, In Inkeles, A., Coleman, J., Smelser, N., eds., *Annual Review of Sociology*, Palo Alto, Cal.: Annual Reviews, Inc., pp. 145-160.
Cromwell, Ronald E., and Olson, David H., eds.
  1975   *Power in Families.* New York: Wiley.
Dahrendorf, Ralf.
  1959   *Class and Conflict in Industrial Society.* Stanford, Cal.: Stanford University Press.
Deutsch, Morton.
  1973   *The Resolution of Conflict.* New Haven, Conn.: Yale University Press.
Duke, James T.
  1976   *Conflict and Power in Social Life.* Provo, Utah: Brigham Young University Press.
Ekeh, Peter P.
  1974   *Social Exchange: The Two Traditions.* Cambridge: Harvard University Press.
Ellis, D.P.
  1971   The Hobbesian problem of order: A critical appraisal of the normative solution. *American Sociological Review* 36:692-703.
Emerson, Richard M.
  1976   Social exchange theory. In Inkeles, A., Coleman, J., Smelser, N., eds., *Annual Review of Sociology.* Palo Alto, Cal.: Annual Reviews, Inc.
Featherman, D.L., and Hauser, R.M.
  1976   Sexual inequalities and socioeconomic achievement in the U.S., 1962-1973. *American Sociological Review* 41:462-483.
File, Karen.
  1975   Final report on data collection for follow-up study. Philadelphia: National Analysts.
Fogarty, Michael P., Rapoport, Rhona, and Rapoport, Robert N.
  1971   *Sex, Career and Family.* Beverly Hills, Cal.: Sage.
Fox, Alan.
  1974   *Beyond Contract: Work, Power and Trust Relations.* London: Faber and Faber.

Gadlin, Howard.
1974   Private lives and public order: A critical view of the history of intimate relations in the U.S. Unpublished paper. Amherst: University of Massachusetts.
Gelles, R.J.
1976   "Abused wives: Why do they stay?" *Journal of Marriage and Family* 38:659-668.
Gerson, Elihu M.
1976   "On 'quality of life.' " *American Sociological Review* 41:793-806.
Glazer-Malbin, N.
1976   "Housework." *Signs* 1:905-922.
Glick, P.C. and Norton, A.J.
1977   Marrying, Divorcing and Living Together in the U.S. Today. *Population Bulletin*, vol. 32, no. 5. Washington, D.C.: Population Reference Bureau.
Goldscheider, Calvin.
1971   *Population, Modernization and Social Structure.* Boston: Little, Brown.
Goode, W.J.
1966   Family disorganization. In Merton, R.K. and Nisbet, R.A., eds., *Contemporary Social Problems.* New York: Harcourt-Brace-Jovanovich, pp. 479-552.
Haug, Marie R.
1973   "Social class measurement and women's occupational roles." *Social Forces* 52:86-98.
Hayghe, H.
1975   Marital and family characteristics of the labor force, March 1974. *Special Labor Force Report 173.* Washington: U.S. Department of Labor Statistics.
Hennig, M. and Jardim, A.
1977   *The Managerial Woman.* New York: Anchor Press/Doubleday.
Hiller, D. and Philliber, W.W.
1978   The derivation of status benefits from occupational attainments of working wives. *Journal of Marriage and Family* 40:63-70.
Heath, Anthony.
1976   *Rational Choice Theory and Social Exchange.* New York: Cambridge University Press.
Holter, Harriet
1970   *Sex Roles and Social Structure.* Oslo: Universitetsforlaget.
Homans, George C.
1974   *Social Behavior: Its Elementary Forms.* 2d ed. New York: Harcourt, Brace, and World.

Re

S It

Kalleberg, A.L.
1977 Work values and job rewards: A theory of job satisfaction. *American Sociological Review* 42:124-143.

Kantor, David, and Lehr, William
1975 *Inside the Family: Toward a Theory of Family Process.* San Francisco: Jossey-Bass.

Kluegel, J.R., Singleton, R. and Starnes, C.E.
1977 Subjective class identification: A multiple indicator approach. *American Sociological Review* 42:599-610.

Knudsen, Dean D.
1975 Response to Reuben Hill. In Johnsen, K.P. ed., *Changing Sex Roles in Marriage.* West Lafayette, Ind.: Institute for Social Change, Monograph No. 5, pp. 32-38.

Komarovsky, Mirra.
1976 *Dilemmas of Masculinity: A Study of College Youth.* New York: W.W. Norton.

Koppel, Ross, and Appelbaum, Eileen
1976 The impact of labor market sex discrimination on the wages and earnings of young women. Paper read at annual meeting of American Sociological Association.

Lamb, Pat
1977 "Lightening up the holidays." *Working Woman* 2:44-47.

Lantz, H.R.
1976 *Marital Incompatibility and Social Change in Early America.* Beverly Hills, Cal.: Sage.

LaRossa, Ralph
1977 *Conflict and Power in Marriage: Expecting the First Child.* Beverly Hills, Cal.: Sage.

Laumann, E.O., and Senter, R.
1976 Subjective social distance, occupational stratification, and forms of status and class-consciousness: A cross-national replication and extension. *American Journal of Sociology* 81:1304-1338.

Levine, Donald N., Carter, E.B., and Gorman, E.M.
1976 Simmel's influence on American sociology, I. *American Journal of Sociology* 81:813-845.

Maret-Havens, Elizabeth.
1977 Developing an index to measure female labor force attachment. *Monthly Labor Review* 100:35-38.

Mason, Karen Oppenheim, Czajka, John, and Arber, Sara.
1976 Change in U.S. Women's sex-role attitudes, 1964-1975. *American Sociological Review* 41:573-596.

McClendon, McKee.
1976 The occupational status attainment processes of males and females. *American Sociological Review* 41:52-64.

Merton, R.K.
   1957   *Social Theory and Social Structure.* New York: Free Press.
Mortimer, J., Hall, R., and Hill, R.
   1976   Husbands' occupational attributes as constraints on wives' employment. Paper read at annual meeting of American Sociological Association.
Noble, Jeanne L.
   1966   The American Negro woman. In Davis, John P., ed., *The American Negro Reference Book.* Englewood Cliffs, N.J.: Prentice-Hall, pp. 522-547.
Nye, F. Ivan.
   1976   *Role Structure and Analysis of the Family.* Beverly Hills, Cal.: Sage.
   1978   Is choice and exchange theory the key? *Journal of Marriage and Family* 40:219-234.
Oakley, Ann.
   1974   *Woman's Work: Housewife Past and Present.* New York: Pantheon.
Oppenheimer, V.K.
   1977   "The sociology of women's economic role in the family." *American Sociological Review* 42:387-405.
Parelius, Ann P.
   1975   Emerging sex role attitudes, expectations, and strains among college women. *Journal of Marriage and Family* 37:146-154.
Park, R.E., and Burgess, E.W.
   1921   *Introduction to the Science of Sociology.* Chicago: University of Chicago Press.
Parnes, H.S., and Nestel, G.
   1975   Factors in career orientation and occupational status. In *Dual Careers.* Vol. 4. Columbus: Center for Human Resource Research, Ohio State University, pp. 57-96.
Pleck, Joseph H.
   1979   Men's new roles in the family: Housework and childcare. In Safiolios-Rothschild, C., ed., *Family and Sex Roles.* Forthcoming.
Pogrebin, L.C.
   1977   Nothing will be the same once you ask the question: Can I change him? *Ms. Magazine* 5 (1):43-47.
Polachek, S.W.
   1975   Discontinuous labor force participation and its effect on women's market earnings. In Lloyd, C.B., ed., *Sex, Discrimination, and the Division of Labor.* New York: Columbia University Press.
Raush, H.L., Barry, W.A., Hertel, R.K., and Swain, M.A.
   1974   *Communication, Conflict, and Marriage.* San Francisco: Jossey-Bass.
Ritter, K.V., and Hargens, L.
   1975   Occupational positions and class identifications of married women: A test of the asymmetry hypothesis. *American Journal of Sociology* 80:964-974.

Rossi, P.H., Sampson, W.A., Bose, C.E., Jasso, G. and Passel, J.
  1974 Measuring household standing. *Social Science Research* 3:169-190.
Rubin, Jeffrey Z., and Brown, Bert R.
  1975 *The Social Psychology of Bargaining and Negotiation.* New York: Academic Press.
Ryder, Norman B., and Westoff, Charles F.
  1971 *Reproduction in the United States, 1965.* Princeton, N.J.: Princeton University Press.
Sampson, W.A., and Rossi, P.H.
  1975 Race and family social standing. *American Sociological Review* 40:201-214.
Scanzoni, John.
  1970 *Opportunity and the Family.* New York: Free Press.
  1972 *Sexual Bargaining: Power Politics in American Marriage.* Englewood Cliffs, N.J.: Prentice-Hall.
  1975a Sex roles, economic factors, and marital solidarity in black and white marriages. *Journal of Marriage and Family* 37:130-145.
  1975b *Sex Roles, Life-Styles, and Childbearing: Changing Patterns in Marriage and Family.* New York: Free Press.
  1976 Sex role change and influences on birth intentions. *Journal of Marriage and Family* 38:43-60.
  1977 *The Black Family in Modern Society: Patterns of Stability and Security.* Chicago: University of Chicago Press (enlarged edition).
  1978 Social processes and power in families. Burr, W.R., Hill, R.H., Nye, F.I., and Reiss, I.L., eds., *Contemporary Theories about Families.* New York: Free Press, pp. 525-568.
  1979a Sex role influences on married women's status attainments. University of North Carolina (Greensboro). Manuscript in preparation.
  1979b Work and fertility control sequences among younger married women. University of North Carolina (Greensboro). Manuscript in preparation.
  1979c Social exchange and behavioral interdependence. Huston, Ted L. and Burgess, Robert L., eds., *Social Exchange and Developing Relationships.* New York: Academic Press.
  1979d An historical perspective on husband-wife bargaining power and marital dissolution. In Levinger, George and Moles, Oliver C., eds., *Divorce and Separation.* New York: Basic Books.
Scanzoni, Letha, and Scanzoni, John.
  1976 *Men, Women, and Change: A Sociology of Marriage and Family.* New York: McGraw-Hill.
Sewell, William H., and Hauser, R.M.
  1975 *Education, Occupation, and Earnings: Achievement in the Early Years.* New York: Academic Press.

Spiegel, J.P.
  1957   The resolution of role conflict within the family. In Williams, R.H.,
         ed., *The Patient and the Mental Hospital.* New York: Free Press, pp.
         545-564.
Sprey, Jetse.
  1969   The family as a system in conflict. *Journal of Marriage and the Family*
         31:699-706.
  1971   On the management of conflict in families. *Journal of Marriage and
         the Family* 33:722-732.
  1972   Family power structure: A critical comment. *Journal of Marriage and
         the Family* 34:235-238.
  1975   Family power and process: Toward a conceptual integration. In
         Cromwell, R.E. and Olson, D.H., eds., *Power in Families.* New York:
         Wiley, pp. 61-79.
Stein, Jess, ed.
  1966   *The Random House Dictionary of the English Language.* New York:
         Random House.
Straus, Murray A.
  1976   Measuring intrafamily conflict and violence: The CRT scales. Univer-
         sity of New Hampshire (Durham), Unpublished paper.
Strauss, A.
  1978   *Negotiations: Varieties, Contexts, Processes and Social Order.* San
         Francisco: Jossey-Bass.
Treiman, D.J., and Terrell, K.
  1975   Sex and the process of status-attainment: A comparison of working
         women and men. *American Sociological Review* 40:174-200.
Turner, Ralph H.
  1964   *The Social Context of Ambition.* San Francisco: Chandler.
U.S. Bureau of the Census, Current Population Reports
  1970   P-60, No. 75.
U.S. Bureau of the Census Current Population Reports
  1975   P-23, No. 54.
U.S. Bureau of the Census, Current Population Reports
  1976   P-20. No. 298.
U.S. Bureau of the Census Current Population Reports
  1977   P-60. No. 105.
U.S. Department of Health, Education and Welfare
  1977   Monthly Vital Statistics Report. Vol. 25. No. 13.
Wallace, Walter, ed.
  1969   *Sociological Theory: An Introduction.* Chicago: Aldine.
Walster, Elaine, and Walster, G.W.
  1975   Equity and social justice. *Journal of Social Issues* 31:21-44.

Westoff, C.F.
1978   Some speculations on the future of marriage and fertility. *Family Planning Perspectives* 10:79-83.
Young, M., and Willomott, P.
1973   *The Symmetrical Family.* London: Routledge, and Kegan Paul.

Index

Index

About the Author

John Scanzoni is professor of sociology and of child relations and family development in The Family Research Center at the University of North Carolina at Greensboro. He was previously at Indiana University for several years. His ongoing research interests over the years have centered on family processes in the context of larger societal forces. Dr. Scanzoni's articles have appeared in professional journals and his books include *Opportunity and the Family* (1970); *Sexual Bargaining* (1972); *Sex Roles, Life-Styles, and Childbearing* (1975); *Men, Women and Change* (with Letha Scanzoni, 1976); and *The Black Family in Modern Society* (1977).